MR. DAVIS'S RICHMOND

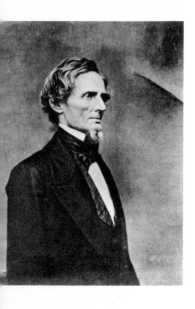

MR. DAVIS'S RICHMOND

Stanley Kimmel

Coward-McCann, Inc.   New York

Books by
Stanley Kimmel

CRUCIFIXION

LEAVES ON THE WATER

THE KINGDOM OF SMOKE

THE MAD BOOTHS OF MARYLAND

MR. LINCOLN'S WASHINGTON

The Bonnie Blue Flag

We are a band of brothers, and native to the soil,
Fighting for the property we gain'd by honest toil;
And when our rights were threaten'd, the cry rose near and far,
Hurrah for the Bonnie Blue Flag, that bears a Single Star!

     Chorus:

Hurrah! Hurrah! for Southern Rights; Hurrah!
Hurrah! for the Bonnie Blue Flag, that bears a Single Star!

As long as the Union was faithful to her trust,
Like friends and like brothers, kind were we and just;
But now, when Northern treachery attempts our rights to mar,
We hoist on high the Bonnie Blue Flag, that bears a Single Star.

     Chorus: Hurrah! etc.

First, gallant South Carolina nobly made the stand;
Then came Alabama, who took her by the hand;
Next, quickly Mississippi, Georgia and Florida,
All rais'd on high the Bonnie Blue Flag that bears a Single Star.

     Chorus: Hurrah! etc.

Ye men of valor, gather round the Banner of the Right,
Texas and fair Louisiana join us in the fight;
Davis, our loved President, and Stephens, Statesman rare,
Now rally round the Bonnie Blue Flag that bears a Single Star.

     Chorus: Hurrah! etc.

And here's to brave Virginia! the Old Dominion State
With the young Confederacy at length has link'd her fate;
Impell'd by her example, now other States prepare
To hoist on high the Bonnie Blue Flag that bears a Single Star.

     Chorus: Hurrah! etc.

Then here's to our Confederacy, strong we are and brave,
Like patriots of old, we'll fight our heritage to save;
And rather than submit to shame, to die we would prefer,
So cheer for the Bonnie Blue Flag that bears a Single Star.

      Chorus: Hurrah! etc.

Then cheer, boys, cheer, raise the joyous shout,
For Arkansas and North Carolina now have both gone out;
And let another rousing cheer for Tennessee be given—
The Single Star of the Bonnie Blue Flag has grown to be Eleven.

      Chorus:

Hurrah! Hurrah! for Southern Rights; hurrah!
Hurrah! for the Bonnie Blue Flag has gain'd th' Eleventh Star!

HARRY MACARTHY

Foreword

MR. DAVIS'S RICHMOND is the story of the Confederate Capital, during the War between the States, as reported by its local press from day to day. Suddenly finding itself overrun by politicians and the military, as well as a host of undesirables, the once peaceful and orderly city was the scene of heroism, pathos, tragedy, laughter and tears. The chronicle of its hectic war years ended with the roar of explosions and a flaming sky as Yankee troops moved in.

The volume follows the same style and arrangement as MR. LINCOLN'S WASHINGTON. It does not attempt to detail history but completes the coverage of events in the capitals of the North and South from 1861 to 1865.

For assistance in locating some of the most important illustrations in MR. DAVIS'S RICHMOND, in addition to the sources mentioned in MR. LINCOLN'S WASHINGTON, acknowledgments are due the Confederate Museum, the Valentine Museum, and the Virginia Historical Society, Richmond, Virginia.

Contents

MR. DAVIS'S RICHMOND

The Man for the Occasion

Guns boomed and crowds cheered wildly as His Excellency, the Honorable Jefferson Davis, President and Commander-in-Chief of the Army and Navy of the Confederate States of America, arrived in Richmond, Virginia, at twenty-five minutes past seven o'clock on the morning of May 29, 1861.

He had traveled from Petersburg on a special train, accompanied by Governor John Letcher of Virginia, Mayor Joseph Mayo of Richmond and members of the City Council, Thomas H. Wynne, Esq., of the House of Delegates, and a number of other gentlemen who had gone there to greet the distinguished representative of Southern rights. Among the President's suite were Colonel Louis T. Wigfall and lady, of Texas, Colonel Joseph R. Davis, brother of the President, and Colonel Lucius Bellinger Northrop, C.S.A.

After the enthusiastic greeting, Mr. Davis was escorted to the carriage waiting for him, by Thomas W. Hoeninger, Esq., of the Spotswood Hotel, and was drawn by four splendid bays to that new and elegantly furnished "traveler's rest" at the corner of Main and Eighth streets. His progress through the streets was marked by deafening shouts of welcome and affectionate demonstrations of popular regard. People rushed up to shake hands with him, some with tears of joy streaming from their eyes.

President Jefferson Davis. *National Archives.*

By the time the carriage arrived at the hotel the crowd had increased to several thousand. Amid the *vivas* of a delighted people, the President ascended the stairs and was conducted to his parlor (No. 83), which had been decorated by Mr. Hoeninger with the coat of arms and the flag of the Confederate States. Mr. Davis hardly had time to get inside of his retreat before he was "vociferously called for," and stepped before an open window to address the citizens of Richmond. Now fifty-three years of age, tall and slender, with the features of a Southern gentleman, he stood erect, his piercing eyes and firm mouth denoting an obstinate disposition. The pointed beard and loosely brushed hair were sandy brown, but the peculiarly curved ears and long nose gave him a rather disdainful appearance. He never failed to give the impression that he had something to say—about himself. His remarks that day, though brief, were to the point and convinced everyone that "Jefferson Davis was the man for the occasion."

Governor Letcher then welcomed "the National ruler to the Metropolis," and was followed by Colonel Wigfall, who proved himself as great on the forum as in the field. In conclusion, several other prominent citizens spoke briefly, and the crowd slowly dispersed. A special breakfast was served, and later Mr. Davis received calls from numerous citizens and government officials. More than 3,000 soldiers were already in the city, making it look like an armed camp. At half past five o'clock that

View of Richmond showing the Spotswood Hotel and Capitol (upper center). *Confederate Museum.*

afternoon, the President reviewed the troops at the Central Fair Grounds, and was "pleased with his men—they with him."

During the day, all stores and government offices had been closed so that employees could join in welcoming the President to the city. With most of the population on the streets, there were many arrests, although the police, vigilant and under the superintendence of the Mayor, attempted to keep the new Capital quiet and in good order. Among those caged (a term used by Richmond reporters for being put in jail) were Reuben, slave of Burwell Jones, for using obscene language in a public place; Peter Allen (white) for getting drunk, and assaulting Robert England in his own home; F. A. Keeper, for urging his team of horses at an unlawful speed on Cary Street; Marie Scott, for attempting to murder Mrs. Ottenheimer's child by throwing her in the river; a soldier from the Second Tennessee Regiment, who had visited the house of a Cyprian, gotten in a "muss," and was stabbed in his leg.

In midtown, a figure was strung up on a lamppost with a card dangling from its shoulders on which was printed in large letters HENRY WARD BEECHER, THE MAN WHO HAS DONE MOST TO CAUSE OUR PRESENT TROUBLE. In one hand was a copy of the New York *Tribune.* The police cut down the figure and burned it. There were many more arrests that day for disorderly behavior, and numerous "suspicious

characters" were then held for investigation.

"As the public knows from the frequent convictions that are daily recorded," the press commented, "the State's prison is unduly crowded with malefactors at this time. The want of room has long been felt as a serious inconvenience, and a drawback on the profitable employment of convict labor. The recent addition to the aggregate of prisoners, caused by the return of the slave transports and free Negroes that have been hired on the railroads, has caused the prison buildings to be more crowded than was either agreeable to the Superintendent or consonant with his labor problems. Unless the Penitentiary buildings are enlarged at no distant day (of which at present there seems not to be the slightest chance) the requirements of the occasion will be such as to demand a full and free use of the Executive prerogative by Governor Letcher."

That day the usual announcements relating to the purchase of Negroes also appeared in Richmond newspapers. One of them reported: "At a sale of a likely lot of Negroes, a girl and boy sold for upwards of $1,200 each, while fellows from 18 to 30 years (field hands) brought from $1,400 to $1,700. This does not indicate any misgivings as to the security of the institution. Old Abe [Lincoln], with all his rail-splitting notoriety, wouldn't sell for half the money in Chicago."

His Honor Mayor Joseph Mayo of Richmond whose difficulties in keeping the Capital quiet and in good order on the day of the President's arrival should have warned him of the troubles to follow. *Cook Collection, Valentine Museum.*

Colonel Lewis T. Wigfall of Texas, one of the most popular speakers of the day. *Library of Congress.*

The Spotswood Hotel Bar, a popular "Rendezvous of Gentlemen." *Harper's Weekly.*

A contemporary cartoon showing "the Dis-United States—a black business." *Library of Congress.*

The Southern press, as well as the military, prepared to repel any and all attacks from the North. On the eve of Fort Sumter, the daily *Richmond Dispatch* had reported: "LATEST NEWS FROM CHARLESTON. April 10, 1861, 10 A.M. The reinforcement of Fort Sumter will be attempted by the U. S. vessels on the flood tide today or tomorrow. The floating battery was put in place, at its final destination, yesterday. Every man in Richmond, capable of bearing arms, is off to the different posts in the harbor. Thousands of soldiers are arriving hourly in trains from the interior. No one doubts Lincoln's policy now. We are amply prepared for him, and there is but one feeling prevailing here, 'Victory or Death!' General Beauregard is in command of all the forces. Major Anderson has acted treacherously, and he will have to take the consequences."

Behind Mr. Davis, and the nation, the gates were closed on any peaceful settlement of internal affairs. Lincoln called out "the militia of the several states of the Union, to the aggregate number of seventy-five thousand in order to suppress said combinations, and to cause the laws to be duly executed." From that time on, events moved swiftly; there was no turning back for the North or the South; the die was cast. Brother took up arms against brother, while the world looked on in amazement at a bloody spectacle endangering a nation which had once fought so valiantly to free itself from the yoke of a foreign tyrant.

Even during the War slave auctions continued to be held.

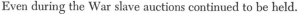

The City of the Seven Hills

Richmond, the City of the Seven Hills, has been described as "the modern Rome." It is about one hundred miles almost directly south of Washington, D. C., on the banks of the James River which gives it an outlet to the Atlantic Ocean, some one hundred and twenty-five miles to the east. The river makes a wide bend before the city, and its banks, during the War between the States, were fringed with factories, mills, and shipping enterprises. The high hills above the river were scattered with homes and many public buildings, for it had three governments to maintain: the city, the State, and the Confederacy.

Founded almost two centuries before Washington, D. C., it had the advantages of permanency long before the Federal Capital was established. Many of its buildings and monu-ments were identified with the history and the growth of the United States. Its capitol had been designed by Thomas Jefferson and was the scene of Aaron Burr's trial for treason. More recently it had been the meeting place of the Virginia secession convention, and was now to witness the sessions of the Confederate Congress. Its rotunda displayed the full-length marble statue of George Washington and the famous bust of the Marquis de Lafayette by Jean Antoine Houdon, prized by the entire nation.

Within the square surrounding the Capitol were the Governor's Mansion, dating from 1811–13; a large equestrian statue of George Washington by Thomas Crawford, an American sculptor; and the Old Bell Tower, once used to call out the militia or the fire brigade

Looking east toward Richmond, across the James River. *Illustrated London News.*

The famous Washington Monument in Capitol Square, Richmond. The steeple to St. Paul's Episcopal Church is seen at the left. *Library of Congress.*

in time of emergency. The statue of Washington, according to Richmond residents, faced toward the South, with its rear to the North, which gave a good idea of what he thought of the Yankees. Directly opposite Capitol Square was St. Paul's Episcopal Church, which the President and his family attended, and elsewhere in the city were other Protestant and Catholic places of worship. The Old Stone House, built in 1737, was the most ancient building in the city, and Mason's Hall, whose cornerstone was laid in 1785, was the oldest exclusively Masonic building in the United States.

The Executive Mansion, dating from 1819, was purchased by the city and leased to the Confederate Government for the occupancy of President Davis during the war years. Remodeling and repairs delayed the family in moving there until late in the summer of 1861. Other landmarks of earlier and happier days for the Union were the former home of Chief Justice John Marshall, built in 1795, and the Valentine home, where Aaron Burr was entertained during his trial.

Main Street was the only real business thoroughfare in the city during the war. Most of the hotels, banks, stores, and newspaper offices were located on or near it. The street extended northward into open country and southward to a suburb called Rocketts. In that dingy neighborhood were several brick buildings joined together, which had been used as tobacco warehouses. They became notorious after being converted into Libby Prison, where thousands of captured Yankees were confined during the war. Overlooking these buildings on one side were the bluffs of Church Hill, which supplied gravel for the city; on the other side were the James River and the Kanawha canal.

Near the summit of Church Hill was another old-fashioned brick building, known as the Almshouse. It had been converted from its original purpose and served as a hospital, attended by the Sisters of Charity. Many former private homes surrounding it also were used as hospitals, some with dirty yellowish flags denoting they were pesthouses for smallpox patients. The mortality in that little community was so great that a hearse was kept in constant requisition, and the streets were shunned by everyone who had no business there.

On the most commanding part of Church Hill was St. John's Church, erected in 1741, which had been the meeting place of the Virginia Convention in 1775. It was there that Patrick Henry uttered his famous "Give me liberty or give me death!" Between this hill and the rickety suburb of Rocketts was a large encampment of Confederate soldiers and batteries along the river for the defense of Richmond. Steamers and sailing craft, which once brought trade to the city, had their mooring places at this point of the river.

Opposite the city, the river enfolded Belle Isle and broke into rapids which provided abundant water power. On this island the government had established another prison for Yankees. At different points, the river was crossed by bridges for vehicles, pedestrians, and railroads. The city had parks and a fairground which were used by the military for parades and drills. Its City Hall, Custom House, hospitals, schools, and other public buildings were ample for its needs before the war, and the old Hollywood Cemetery—where James Monroe, fifth President of the United States, was buried—took care of its hereafter.

Front view of the Confederate Capitol, Richmond. *Confederate Museum.*

The Old Bell Tower in Capitol Square, Richmond. *Library of Congress.*

When the shadows of war fell over Richmond, it quickly became filled with military leaders, politicians, and denizens of the underworld. The tide and type of its growing population resembled Washington, the capital of the United States. Troops from other Southern states were arriving, being mustered into service, drilling in the streets, vacant lots, military parade grounds, and other open spaces. The people were proud of their city's history, and the fact that it was the Capital of Virginia and the Capital of the Confederate States. They shouted, cursed, and boasted they could shoot better than their Yankee enemies. "Victory or Death!" they cried while the bands played, women wept, and men went out to the slaughter of the booming guns.

The selection of Richmond as the Capital of the Confederate States gave residents a feeling of great importance, and the promise of a thriving metropolis in the near future.

St. Paul's Episcopal Church, Richmond, opposite Capitol Square, was attended by President Davis and his family. *Cook Collection, Valentine Museum.*

"The Confederate Government is in Richmond," said the press. "It has come to make its *home* with us during our struggle with the North. It could not bear the discomfort of living so remote as Montgomery from the seat of danger and the theater of the campaign. It could not brook the idea of being itself secure, while Virginia was in danger. It desired to meet the enemy face to face. It wished to plant itself in the very heat and heart of the battle—its toe to the foe. It would not consent, like that prudent captain in the fable, to bid the gallant troops of the Confederacy *go* and fight. It preferred to say, *come* and do battle with us. It longed to be in the very midst of events, in the bosom of the army. It has done wisely; it has behaved gallantly; Virginia welcomes it with outstretched arms and swelling hearts.

"President Davis is here, worn with labor, but nerved to the high duties of his respon-

The Governor's Mansion in Capitol Square, Richmond. *Confederate Museum.*

Two views of Main Street, Richmond, the one on the left from a contemporary photograph. During the War between the States, most of the business establishments were located there. *Library of Congress.*

The historic Valentine House (center) in Richmond, now the Valentine Museum. *Valentine Museum.*

The Richmond City Hall. "Mayor's Court up one Flight." *Virginia Historical Society.*

The Almshouse, fronting on one of the old graveyards where many smallpox victims were buried. *National Park Service.*

St. John's Church, an early place of worship in Richmond. Note boys wearing Confederate uniforms and wagon used for carrying hospital supplies. *Library of Congress.*

The Old Stone House, most ancient of all buildings in Richmond. *Valentine Museum.*

great States, ten powerful and indomitable allies that present themselves in their persons upon her soil. Mr. Howell Cobb, President of the first Confederate Congress, in a speech at Atlanta, has eloquently explained the motive which actuated the men at Montgomery in coming to Richmond.

" 'If you wish to know why the Government was removed to Richmond, I can say, circumstances have arisen that have rendered it proper. We have received the Old Dominion into our Confederacy. Her soil will, perhaps, be the battle ground of this struggle. Her enemies are gathered around her to force her into subjection to their foul dictates. We felt it our duty to be at the seat of war. We wanted to let Virginia know that whatever threats or dangers were presented to her, filled our hearts with sympathy for her, which we are willing to exhibit, to show that there was not a man in the Confederacy who was afraid to be at his post on Virginia soil. We also wanted to be near our brave boys, so that when we threw off the badge of Legislators, we might take up arms and share with them the fortunes of war. We felt the cause of Virginia to be the cause of us all. If she falls, we shall all fall; and we are willing to be at the spot to be among the first victims. We are ready to say to Lincoln,

sible position. The spacious mansion of Mr. Crenshaw, at Clay and Twelfth streets, the one built by Dr. Brockenbrough, has been taken for his residence. This is to be the White House of the South. There will be his gifted lady, not less talented and intellectual than himself, to dispense the refined hospitalities which befit the residence of the chief man and loftiest statesman of all the South. Richmond may felicitate herself upon the acquisition she has made, in the families of the President and Cabinet, to her social and fashionable circles.

"The people of Virginia will appreciate this advent of the Southern Government to her own metropolis. It is a pledge, the very highest which the South could give of the purpose which actuates her in this struggle. It is not merely a President and Cabinet, but it is ten

24

A group of tobacco warehouses near the river were converted into the notorious Libby Prison where captured Yankees were confined during the War. *Library of Congress*.

Unloading grain at one of the busy landing places in the Richmond suburb of Rocketts. *National Archives*.

when he attempts to put his foot on Virginia soil, "thus far shalt thou come, and no farther!"'

"The presence of the Confederate Government, backed by all the power of the Southern States, and supported by the hundreds of regiments now on their way to Virginia, will put our safety beyond peradventure, whatever be the force General Scott may throw into Virginia. We shall soon assume the offensive. Our regiments will soon be *at* the enemy and be *after* him. It is well to accustom our men for a little while to the presence of the opposing forces, and to indoctrinate them in warfare by skirmishes and sallies. It is well to ascertain by a brief practice of the Fabian policy the designs and plans of the enemy. It is well to let him penetrate somewhat into the interior in order that when we do strike he may be the more completely in our power. It is well to allow as large forces as possible to accumulate around our standards before decisive measures are taken. It is well that the Confederate Government should become a little familiar with the field and with the position of affairs before the war is opened in earnest. Delays are not dangerous in war when they are employed by the masters of strategy.

"We feel implicit confidence in the ability of the Government and its Generals. Educated at West Point to the profession of arms, schooled to active war in the campaigns of Mexico, familiarized with the manipulations of troops and with the mechanism of army organization by four years experience in the Department of War at Washington, President Davis, of all the men of the South, is probably the most thoroughly qualified for the duties of Commander-in-Chief in the present contest. His high personal traits of character, his iron will, his indomitable spirit, his tried courage, his laborious habits of business, his mastery of details, his propensity to do *thoroughly* whatever he undertakes at all, his temperance, his

Street entrance to the President's Mansion with stables and carriage house at right. *Confederate Museum.*

Mr. Howell Cobb, President of the First Confederate Congress. *Valentine Museum.*

prudence, his wisdom, his unselfishness, his piety, his freedom from all partisan asperity and all partisan chicanery, his amiable and catholic temper, which extorted the respect and admiration of the most violent abolition curs in the Senate at Washington—all these qualities mark President Davis out, not merely as the chosen of the people for the grave responsibilities of his present position, but as the instrument of Providence for accomplish-

ing its own beneficent designs. It is impossible that the South should not feel secure with such a man as this at the helm; and thrice welcome is he to Richmond, where all respect, admire, and confide in him."

Other Confederate leaders had previously arrived in Richmond. In April, Robert Edward Lee was cheered upon his return there and escorted to the same Spotswood Hotel where crowds had called for him and he had responded saying that he "pledged himself to the performance of his duty and to the land of his birth." He was fifty-four years old, and had just been appointed Major General, commanding the military forces of Virginia. Everyone who greeted him felt that his presence acted with majestic influence on all the citizens, for they realized that in him they had a prize of no ordinary magnitude. Before leaving Washington, he had resigned from the United States army, and had his last interview with General-in-Chief Winfield Scott, who had said: "It would be better for every officer in the [United States] army, including myself, to die, than Colonel Robert E. Lee." The Honorable Alexander H. Stephens, Vice-President of the Confederacy, was at the Exchange Hotel, and had conferred with Lee and Governor John Letcher concerning Virginia's secession on April 17, the day before Lee's arrival.

By the end of May, ten states had seceded from the Union: South Carolina, Mississippi, Florida, Alabama, Georgia, Louisiana, Texas, Virginia, Arkansas, and North Carolina. The Confederate flag, however, then had but seven

Lee and his Generals. (left to right) John B. Hood, Richard Stoddert Ewell, Braxton Bragg, Albert Sidney Johnston, Wade Hampton, E. Kirby Smith, Jubal A. Early, A. P. Hill, S. D. Lee, Richard H. Anderson, John B. Gordon, Theophatos S. Holmes, William Hardee, Joseph E. Johnston, Simon B. Buckner, James Longstreet, Leonidas Polk, R. E. Lee, N. B. Forrest, P. G. T. Beauregard, Thomas J. Jackson, Samuel Cooper, J. E. B. Stuart, Richard Taylor, J. C. Pemberton, D. H. Hill. *National Park Service.*

stars in its circle, denoting the original states to secede, and their people anxiously awaited news that more than ten of the fifteen Southern states would join them. Only one, Tennessee, was to follow their example, which made up the eleven stars in the flag that finally represented the Confederacy.

After celebrating Mr. Davis's arrival, Richmond resumed its usual activities. All places of business were open and shoppers were on a spending spree. Merchants were offering complete stocks of spring and summer goods: black silk mantles, bonnets, ruche, plain and figured grenadine, barege, ribbons, satins, velvets, challie, poplin, "at prices to suit the times which, for variety and style cannot be excelled anywhere." Miss Rebecca Seymore was exhibiting her new and elegant styles of the Paris fashions for ladies and children at showrooms in her residence. Charles Langley had a sign over the entrance to his tinshop which read: NO YANKEE HUMBUG. BRASS LETTERS FOR MILITARY CAPS MADE TO ORDER. COMPANIES FURNISHED VERY CHEAP. Bookshop windows displayed Colonel William S. Hardee's *Rifle*

and Light Infantry Tactics, and *The Volunteer's Handbook,* by Captain James K. Lee, with a note stating that both books were published in the South. "The Confederate March," with a likeness of Mr. Davis and the new Confederate flag on the title page, was on sale everywhere, price fifty cents.

Dr. M. A. Schlosser was at the Spotswood Hotel, where Mr. Davis was living. The doctor was internationally famous for curing diseases of the feet, such as bunions and corns. In his advertisements he announced that he had treated Napoleon III, the King of Bavaria, Prince Richard Metternich, the Archduke of Austria, and a score of other European notables. N. Blaid & Company had on hand several choice brands of mountain whiskey: "All who wish the pure article will do well to give us a call." The City Council had just ordered hotelkeepers, proprietors of restaurants, saloons, and all other places where "ardent spirits, porter, beer or cider is sold or given away" to close every night at ten. Otherwise, "Fine $20. Every day considered a separate offense."

"We feel implicit confidence in the ability of the government and its generals." *Valentine Museum.*

29

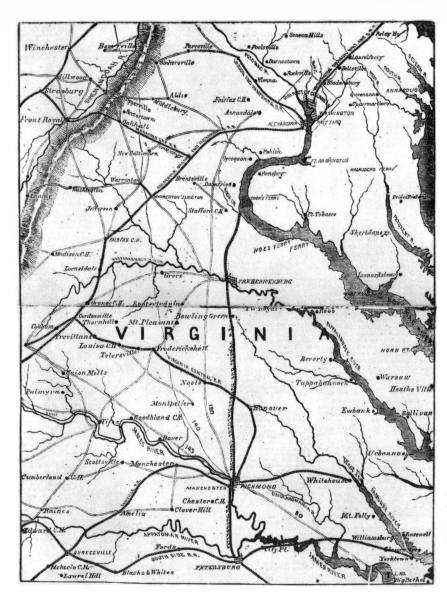

Map of the War in eastern Virginia (left) and a bird's-eye view of forts and encampments in the vicinity of Richmond (below). *Frank Leslie's Illustrated Newspaper* and *Harper's Magazine*.

Confederate troops arriving outside the city of Richmond. *Valentine Museum.*

A Confederate regiment marches through Capitol Square on the way to join other forces at the front. *Harper's Weekly.*

The city surrounded by troops. An encampment on Belle Isle. *National Archives.*

Confederate soldiers practicing with bowie knives at a camp near Richmond. *Harper's Weekly*.

Manufacturers were turning out pianos, stoves, ranges, furnaces, and a variety of home appliances. "Even the exigencies of an active state of hostilities cannot wholly repress the business energies of the Richmond people," commented the press. "A number of homes and buildings are going up in different sections of the city, and a scarcity of material is not apprehended."

The announcement that Mr. Davis would receive visitors at the Governor's Mansion gave many residents an opportunity to meet him personally. The reception of ladies was from eleven to twelve, and of gentlemen from twelve to half-past one o'clock. Many supposed that Mrs. Abraham Lincoln's brother, David H. Todd, would attend, but they were disappointed. Todd had been commissioned a lieutenant in the army of the Confederate States, and was on military duty in North Carolina. The report was circulated, however, that he had said before leaving Richmond that he desired nothing more ardently than to scalp his sister's husband.

But Lieutenant Todd should have joined the Texas Rangers, who had recently come to Richmond, if he so ardently desired to carry out that operation. They had volunteered their services to the Confederate army and were regarded by all who had seen them drill and perform their feats of skill on the streets and parade grounds in the city as the greatest horsemen in the world. They excelled in the use of bowie knives, had fought Indians, and could—riding at full speed—lift a man from the ground, scalp him, and throw him away without lessening the onrush of the horse. Although dummies were used in such exhibitions, it was generally acknowledged that if attached to Confederate infantry they would be of great service in border actions against the Yankees. Under the title "A Sagacious Horse," one reporter wrote: "The Texas Rangers can do anything that can be done on a horse. We saw one on the street yesterday that knew all the cavalry commands, and performed all the movements as the rider called them out. After the drill, the Ranger asked him what he would do with the Yankees, and he replied by leaping on the ground as a deer leaps on a poisonous snake."

Appointments from civil life into the regular army had been indefinitely suspended, but calls for all available fighting men as volunteers were being made: "WANTED—Virginia Guard: Twenty more men for this company, now in service. Apply to the recruiting Sergeant, at the office of Bayly & White, Attorneys-at-Law, at the corner of Twelfth and Franklin streets. By order of Capt. Saml. T. Bayly. WANTED—A trumpeter for one of the Light Artillery Companies stationed at the Baptist College. A young man of steady habits will be received and mustered in at once. Pay $12 per month, with clothing and subsistence. Apply to the Commanding Officer, Baptist College. WANTED—Volunteers for the Jackson Guard. Uniform complete, of the best material, furnished free. Headquarters, Front room under the St. Charles Hotel. H. B. Dickson, Captain. WANTED—Recruiting: Sound, able-bodied MEN for the Army of the Confederate States. A premium of TWO DOLLARS for each recruit will be paid to citizens who will bring them to my rendezvous, and the cost of transportation from the residence of the recruit to Richmond (within fifty miles), by railway or canal, will be paid. The requirement for recruits: that they shall be free white men, between the ages of eighteen and thirty-five; at least five feet four and a half inches high;

sound, able bodied, and of good character. Those who may be desirous of forwarding recruits, will communicate with me without delay. A recruit receives eleven dollars a month, clothing and rations. For further information, inquire at my office on Bank street in the old Madison House, next door to the Custom House. John Scott, Capt. C.S.A. Recruiting Officer."

Animals and equipment also came under the same heading: "WANTED—1,000 mules for the State of Virginia. No. 1 mules from 14 to 15½ inches high, and from four to eight years old. They must be sound and well broken, for which cash will be paid on delivery. B. F. Ficklin, Quartermaster General. WANTED—For Quartermaster's Department, 500 good serviceable HORSES for artillery use. No horses may be offered but those which are perfectly sound in every respect; also, 250,000 lbs. HAY; 500,000 lbs. STRAW; 15,000 bushels CORN; and 20,000 bushels OATS. W. S. Wood, Assistant Quartermaster. WANTED — Ordnance Department: Sealed proposals for altering 5,000 flint-lock muskets with percussion. 5,000 best rifle muskets—calibre, English or American 57 or 58. 2,000 best revolver pistols, Navy or Army size.

Recruiting for the Confederate Army. *Harper's Weekly.*

The Female Institute, Richmond, was used as the Quartermaster's Office during the War. *National Archives.*

The Confederate Army Hay Depot at Rocketts Landing near Libby Prison (at left). *National Archives.*

1,000 cavalry carbines, breach-loading, Army size. 1,000 light cavalry sabers, Battery wagons, Howitzers, traveling forges, haversacks, axes, spades, tents, mess pans, canteens, bayonets, belts, etc."

Notices also appeared advising those in the service of military activities: "Headquarters, Fry's Mounted Rangers. Attention Rangers! Assemble for drill in the Valley, near Victor's Mill, this evening at 4½ o'clock. Those members unprovided with horses will be drilled on foot. By order of Capt. Caskie. General Headquarters—Adjutant General's Office: In all cases where Brigadier Generals of the Militia have accepted commissions in the Active Volunteer Force, or in the Provisional Army of the States, the Senior Colonels will forthwith assume command of the Brigades, and cause the returns to be made as required by law. Arms, accouterments, and ammunition can only be issued upon the order of Major General Lee. All certificates of election of officers, and other matters connected with the Militia force not in service, must, as heretofore, be addressed to this office. By command, W. H. Richardson, Adjutant General."

The First Virginia Cavalry comes to a halt and awaits orders near a battlefield. *Harper's Weekly.*

The ladies of Richmond were asked to bear in mind that they could add materially to the comfort of soldiers in the hospitals and at nearby camps of instruction by sending them baked custards, eggs, milk, and other provisions. Also, if they would search out the wives and mothers of volunteers in the Confederate army, who were ill provided for because they were too proud to make their own wants known, and give them sewing or other employment, they would be doing a great deal of good.

Newspapers were filled with reports of the arrival and departure of troops. Soldiers, in the city for so short a time, often were reckless in their use of firearms. "Too much precaution cannot be exercised in such matters," warned the press. "Several soldiers, passing by the home of John C. Sinton fired at a post with their muskets. They missed the post but hit and killed Mr. Sinton's horse, worth $300. The horse deserved a better fate than to fall victim to such reckless conduct."

Work on the city railway was progressing, though it was hardly possible that it would be finished during the summer. A citizen, looking at the laborers on Main Street, asked why so many were imported from the North while Richmond men were out of employment.

Steamboats and shipping lines were announcing a change in schedules for the season, and resorts such as White Sulphur Springs were advertising retreats for families from the present excitement secure from attack either by land or water.

Trains were still carrying passengers and mail between Richmond, Washington, Philadelphia, and New York, but, since no tickets would be sold to servants [slaves], those wishing to travel had to have some responsible white person, known to the officials of the railroad companies, obtain passage for them. At the same time, the Adams Express Company advertised that it would forward slaves in charge of careful and reliable messengers.

Davis, Deupree & Company were giving their entire attention to the sale of Negroes, publicly and privately, at the Odd Fellows Hall, corner of Mayo and Franklin streets, the owners of the company being listed as

View of the James River Canal and Confederate troops on their way to western Virginia. *Harper's Weekly.*

Ro. H. Davis, Wm. S. Deupree, and S. R. Fondren. Among the WANTED advertisements in one newspaper was: "I wish to buy a boy from 9 to 11 years old. One of good character. Cash will be paid. E. D. Eacho." Another read: "FOR SALE PRIVATELY—A valuable young WOMAN, about 20 years of age, sound and healthy. She is a very good Cook, Washer, and Ironer, a splendid House Servant, and an Excellent Seamstress. She is one of the most valuable servants I know. Apply to P. F. White, corner 3rd and Byrd streets." Under LOCAL MATTERS was this: "LOST—MY FREE PAPERS. They were in a leather pocketbook. I will give $1 reward for them if left at this newspaper office. Lucy Ellan Robertson. A free woman of color."

Rewards for runaway slaves were listed, generally, with small figures to denote male or female: "$25 REWARD—Runaway, on the 29th of March, a woman named NANCY, whom I purchased of H. Stern, of this city. She is of medium size, rather spare made, of a gingerbread color, has a diffident look when spoken to, is about twenty-three years old and has a

blister scar on her neck. She was sold last Christmas at the sale of Wm. Andrews, dec'd, nine miles above the city. She may now be in the neighborhood, or near Slash Cottage, as she has a mother living at Mr. Wm. Winns, near that place, in Hanover County. She was hired to Mr. Samuel Allen, of this city, last year, and has a husband hired to Mr. Ballard, at the Exchange Hotel, by the name of Dolphins. I will pay the above reward if delivered to me in Richmond. R. B. Woodward."

"FIVE DOLLARS REWARD—Runaway, ELIZA, a slave, property of R. W. Thompson, Esq., about 35 years old, of medium size, dark brown skin; has a burn or scar on one of her cheeks, and lisps when speaking. She may probably be found at the house of her sister, Fanny White, on 7th, north of Broad street, in this city. The above reward will be promptly paid for her delivery to B. A. Cocks at the Exchange Hotel."

"Runaway—In jail, a Negro calling himself JOHN FORD, as a runaway but who claims to be a free man. The owner of said Negro is requested to come forward, prove property, pay charges and take him away, else he will be dealt with as the law directs and sold. C. S. Chisholme, Acting Jailer."

A gang of some forty runaways were discovered in a camp near a place called Catfish swamp within the city limits. The camp was broken up by members of the Richmond Vigilante Committee and eight of the runaways were captured. They also were being held for identification. Masters who had slaves at large were warned to make certain they were not in the lot, for all not claimed would be sold at the next auction.

In the eyes of the white people, to be a free Negro was, according to the Richmond press, to be idle, trifling, and good for nothing. The judgment was harsh, the press admitted, but valid on the principle that the majority of a class gives tone and direction to the whole. "The Mayor said yesterday in his court-room," wrote a reporter, "that not one-tenth of the free negro population of Richmond were charged with tithables, which one can well believe, knowing their universal objection to physical exertion, by which alone they could acquire sustenance. The police are, very properly, we think, bringing before the Mayor all free negroes who have not paid their taxes. Such parties will no doubt be committed as vagrants, and set to work either on projected fortifications for city defense or on the various streets that may need repairing during the summer months. Yesterday, John King, free negro, was brought up for nonpayment of his taxes and committed as a vagrant. Bill Graves was committed for going about

Notices of Negro sales and rewards for runaway slaves were common throughout the South until the end of the War. *Richmond Dispatch.*

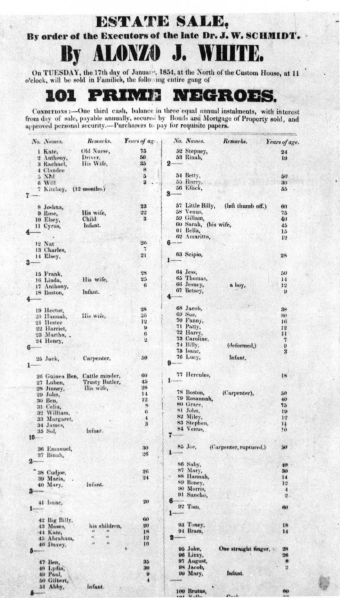

Camp of Negro refugees hiding out near Richmond. *Harper's Weekly.*

without a certificate of his freedom. Scott Harris, Joe Gilpin, and Kitt Scott were lectured as vagrants, and it is believed sent to jail, as the officers started with some half dozen colored subjects to the lockup."

The Mayor was trying to clear the city of lazy free Negroes and slaves who had found their way to the Capital "for the purpose of accumulating a subsistence by practicing the art of doing a great deal of nothing." These cases brought before him were typical of others: A free Negro from Powhatan county, calling himself Grandison Smith, was committed to jail and punished with stripes [whipped] for having no register of his freedom. Anderson, a runaway slave belonging to James Jones, of Petersburg, was ordered to receive twenty lashes, and to be kept in jail until legally taken out. A juvenile Negro named Henry, the property of Mrs. Maria Thrift, was sentenced to twenty-five lashes for breaking into Payton Walden's house and committed to jail as a runaway. "Henry's neck was ornamented with an iron collar and a padlock, which led to the inference that he was a youth of very bad propensities."

Mary Holmes, a Negro woman committed to jail as a runaway, was ordered to be sold and the proceeds placed in the state treasury, according to the provisions of section 19 of Chapter 105 of the Code, nobody having laid

claim to her. Washington Brown, colored, who remained in Virginia contrary to law, was tried and ordered to be sold into slavery. One Negro fared better: Dick Bird, a free man of color, was arraigned before the Mayor for being in the city contrary to law. He proved that he belonged to the Sixth North Carolina regiment and was let off.

There were many strict laws for Negroes which the Mayor also was trying to enforce. George, a slave of John Freeman, was sentenced to fifteen lashes for going out at night without a pass. Lewis, a slave, the property of Crump & Jenkins, was awarded several stripes for roaming at large, a circumstance which led to the suspicion that he was a runaway. Robert Lumpkin's Negro Timothy was punished in the usual way for smoking a cigar on the street. R. W. Oliver's Negro hack driver, for refusing, when not engaged otherwise, to carry a white person demanding his services, was ordered to be whipped. Isaac Travis, a free Negro, and Aurelius, a slave, were ordered to be whipped for fighting. A white woman, Julia Washman, was charged with selling ardent spirits to a slave without the permission of his owner; her license for keeping an ordinary (a tavern) was revoked. Peter, a slave of P. B. Stanard, Captain of the Thomas Artillery, brought before the Mayor for carrying a concealed weapon, said he carried it by reason of his connection with the military. He was ordered returned to his master. The Mayor read the ordinance dealing with slaves and masters and said it was important that restrictions should be thrown around abuses of it under present conditions; especially was it wrong to deal with Negroes so extensively in liquor and matches.

Some cases had to do with "itchy fingers." William, slave of J. H. May, was sentenced to twenty-five lashes by the Mayor for appropriating two vests belonging to John Campbell without his consent or knowledge. Morgan, slave of Frank Whitlock, was given fifteen lashes for stealing a bucket of honey from Henry Mosby. John, slave of George W. Gretter, charged with stealing two canteens of whiskey from his master, was sent down under sentence of thirty-nine lashes. Elijah, slave of Stephen Hunter, was tried for breaking into James H. Beagleston's store and stealing a large lot of groceries. He was convicted and sentenced to receive thirty-nine lashes, "well laid on."

Summer rains retarded many activities in 1861, including business and the growing of crops needed by the people of Richmond and the army in their midst. The James River had risen six or seven feet and was still moving upward. Mayo's Island, at the mouth of the toll bridge, was nearly overflowing, but, owing to timely precautions, none of the lumber owned by Messrs. John and George Gibson, who had a sawmill there, was lost. Sundry animals were drowned, and a cow, alive and kicking, floated past Mayo's bridge, an unwilling voyager unable to extricate itself from the whirling flood. The wharves at Rocketts were submerged, the surplus water covering the streets without doing any particular damage to property. A large quantity of driftwood floated off from the low grounds bordering the James River above and below the city, and some vessels at the wharves required extra moorings to prevent them from being carried away by the flood. Shockoe Creek was surging and boiling in an unusual manner. Many cellars in the lower part of the city were filled with water and goods damaged. Vauxhall was still above ground.

The flood was at its greatest height one evening when a large portion of Rocketts was under water, the tide bringing it up to the rear of several stores. The inconvenience experienced by citizens residing in that part of the city was much increased by the heavy volume of water forced back by the inflowing tide. A woman and two children in one of the houses which was filling with water made a very narrow escape from drowning while endeavoring to reach dry land; the stout arms and willing hearts of their neighbors saved them from a watery grave. The Central Railroad sustained such serious damage that the mails did not leave by that route for several days, the earth having been washed away very badly in places along its line of travel. The Fredericksburg Railroad also was damaged.

Many farmers complained that the water had destroyed their crops by overflowing their lands, besides carrying away bridges, mills, dams, and drowning cattle. The Chickahominy bridge was washed away, and the freshet was higher at the "swamp" than it was known to have been for forty years. The turnpike lowgrounds and all other places capable of retaining water were inundated. All farming operations were suspended; no corn was planted and all the flatland wheat was submerged several feet. The entire Brook stream covered the whole flat from hill to hill, some three quarters of a mile wide. The strong stone abutment bridge over the stream crossing Bacon Quarter branch had been washed away to such an extent that it was unfit for use when the water subsided. These lands were to be overrun in the near future with more than water.

The "dandy slave" was the envy of all household servants. *Illustrated London News.*

Notwithstanding the growing difficulties of supplying food and other provisions for the army, the currency problems of the new Confederacy, a Federal blockade of 3,000 miles of coastline against the export of cotton and the import of needed materials, and a lack of naval power, the new government dived into a war whose currents were to take it into a whirlpool of extinction. And their boast at the beginning, that the South had never been successfully invaded, was to be short-lived.

The people were informed that the possibility of any enemy conquering or plundering their lands was almost nil, due not only to the climate (which made campaigning in summer as impracticable as in winter), but also to the great distances, the many large watercourses crossing roads and highways, their own warlike character, and the incorruptible fidelity of the slaves. The South, it was noted, had a seaboard and such breadth of swamp and sand that it could be invaded only from the Chesapeake, from Charleston, from New Orleans, or from the upper Mississippi.

From the Chesapeake, only Eastern Virginia could be assailed, they were told; any attempt to reach North Carolina or distant parts of the interior would require long lines of communication, crossing wide rivers, which readily could be broken up. Charleston was closed by impregnable forts; New Orleans protected by its distance, its miasma, and its boundless swamps and canebrakes. In fact, all the South was secure from invasion except Eastern Virginia and therefore could afford to concentrate its forces in Virginia. These forces, the people were reminded, were now pouring in upon the state in formidable numbers, and the cause was safe. In addition, the presence of the Confederate Government in Richmond was equivalent to a host of men. The excellent generalship of President Davis would soon infuse system, order, and confidence in every division and corps. When such forces were well in hand and all things ready for the fray, the people would see what fate awaited the invaders of Virginia. It was plainly evident, said their military leaders, that while the South was closed, the North was very open to invasion and, if the war lasted a year, it would be waged upon Northern soil. The Virginia campaign would make veterans of the Southern forces; it would be for them to assume the offensive. In elation the patriots cried, "We shall carry the war into Africa; we shall commend the chalice prepared for us to their own lips!"

Before sundown on May 30, 1861, a Confederate soldier was writing home: "We are now one hundred and fifty miles further than the first place we stopped at. The Yankees have taken one of our towns—Alexandria. We are expecting a fight any minute. Ten thousand of Lincoln's men have marched in there, and six hundred of our men had to leave. We have now in camp about twenty-seven hundred men."

With President Davis safely established in Richmond, authorities of the Confederate States made preparations for setting up the machinery of the government there. Buildings suited for the various departments were engaged and workmen began fitting them up for use. Attention was called to the tardiness in work on the city defenses and notices were published requesting all citizens, since speed was desirable, to report immediately to the Mayor or the committee in charge of the work what labor or digging or wheeling tools they could spare. The tools were needed for a large group of free Negroes who had appeared at the City Hall to enroll as workers on the fortifications. They were informed that at the conclusion of each day's work they could come into the city if they saw fit. If they answered promptly to the roll call, they would be fed and paid; if not, they would get something else. What that was the Mayor, who was spokesman for the committee, did not say.

Apparently the Negroes followed the Mayor's advice, for every evening, after coming into the city, they marched back to their quarters with smiling faces and drums beating which, said a reporter, did "not betoken, by any means, that they were displeased in contributing toward defending their native soil from foreign invaders."

Notices appeared in the Richmond press that Commissioners of the Confederate States,

Our Best Harbor Defences—Cotton Bales. Jonathan—"Now, Father John, come and take 'em as per invoice." *Frank Leslie's Illustrated Newspaper.*

A "Smash" for the President of the Confederate States—made with fire-water. *Frank Leslie's Illustrated Newspaper.*

The Confederate privateer and blockade runner *Sumter* taking on coal at an island in the Caribbean Sea. *Frank Leslie's Illustrated Newspaper.*

Negroes at work on the fortifications defending the Capital. *Illustrated London News.*

appointed by the city, were prepared to accept subscriptions to the loan authorized by the act of Congress for investment in bonds (coupons or registered, as the subscribers preferred), which were secured by a specific export duty on cotton, and would bear 8 per cent interest, payable half yearly. From the beginning, the people had little faith in the finances of the Confederate Government. Congress shifted from one scheme to another in an effort to establish its pecuniary resources, but the blockade made them all in-

effective for any long period. With an army, and thousands of civilians in its various departments, the government was at all times hard pressed for cash.

Some of the "patriots" who had recently come to Richmond in search of employment were accused of having held on to the Lincoln regime in Washington as long as safety permitted. That such characters should succeed angered one reporter who "walked the rounds to look them over." What he saw in general, however, convinced him that there was enough clerical force employed in the several departments to make one or two very fine battalions of "Government Zouaves." He confessed that he had never seen "such violent attempts to do nothing for good pay" on the part of so large and respectable a body of his own quill-driving friends as he witnessed on his rambles. "The sight was instructive, if not amusing," he commented. "Everybody should have a Government job."

The arrival of General Pierre Gustave Toutant Beauregard in Richmond on the last day of May created great excitement. The Capital of the Confederate States could boast that it now had, within its confines, President Jefferson Davis, Generals Robert E. Lee, Beauregard and Albert Sidney Johnston, Colonel (later General) John Bankhead Magruder, and others—the most brilliant military men of the American continent. Hundreds of citizens and soldiers greeted the distinguished general as he emerged from the Petersburg train and hurried through the crowd to a private carriage which was to take him to his headquarters at the Exchange Hotel. People surrounded the vehicle, cheered, shook his hand, or seemed satisfied to touch even the "hem of his garment." Modestly acknowledging the demonstrations, he avoided them as soon as possible and drove off while the cheering crowd made way for his carriage. At the Spotswood Hotel, he stopped for a moment to pay his compliments to the President, but,

President Davis and Christopher G. Memminger, Confederate Secretary of the Treasury, "hang on for dear life." *Frank Leslie's Illustrated Newspaper.*

Mr. Davis being absent, he proceeded on his way to his own hotel. After inspecting his quarters there, he was greeted at an informal reception attended by many prominent men in the Confederacy.

The venerable ex-President of the United States, John Tyler, now a member of the provisional Confederate Congress, was also in the city. He was described as being in the enjoyment of most excellent health and spirits "despite the fact that his mansion and grounds [at Hampton, Virginia] have been stolen by Lincoln's minions and a foreign flag raised over them."

Joining others in the news was "Double Block," from the crew of the Confederate steamer *Yorktown,* who was visiting Richmond friends. He was famous as the "Captain" of the rifle cannon at Charleston which had battered the walls of Fort Sumter. "It was confessed by Major Anderson and his Yankee comrades that 'Double Block' knows how to load and point a gun," wrote a reporter. "We hope he may have an opportunity 'some of these days' to try his hand again."

Two local press items related to the President and his lady. At a patriotic gathering, Mr. Morton, a Richmond florist, presented Mrs. Davis with a magnificent bouquet, composed of the choicest flowers of the greenhouse and garden. She accepted the offering and returned thanks for it, saying it was the most beautiful she ever had received. Mr. Davis fared somewhat better. Brigadier General John B. Floyd and a few gentlemen of the city presented him with an elegant pair of horses, blood-bay in color, excellently matched, young and finely formed, and valued at one thousand dollars.

The President had announced that June 13, 1861, would be set aside as a day of fasting and prayer to be observed in all the Confederate states. Such observances were to follow at intervals throughout the war. On that day government offices, stores, and amusement places were closed in Richmond, and the people attended church services throughout the city. As if in answer to their supplications, they read the first newspaper reports: GLORIOUS VICTORY—BATTLE OF BETHEL CHURCH—GALLANT

John Tyler, former President of the United States (1841–1845), served as a member of the provisional Confederate Congress. *National Archives.*

General Pierre G. T. Beauregard, Confederate hero. *National Archives*.

Mrs. Jefferson Davis as the First Lady of the South. From a portrait in the Confederate Museum.

A Richmond, Fredericksburg, and Potomac Railroad train rumbles through a street in the Capital. *Frank Leslie's Illustrated Newspaper.*

Several weeks before, some three hundred Federal soldiers had occupied Bethel Church, near Fortress Monroe, and upon leaving had written on its walls "Death To The Traitors! Down With The Rebels!" Enraged by such blasphemy, Colonel Magruder determined to put an end to such excursions into the interior of Virginia and filled the place with his own men. But a much larger force of Yankees, under Major General Benjamin F. Butler, returned and the fight was on. The result might have been explained by the remark of a Confederate soldier who said that "the Yankees fired very badly. Lieut. Gregory was on horseback, and the balls [shots] whizzed far above his head."

Three other soldiers, racing to the body of a dead Yankee, found on him a fine dress sword, a watch, side arms, and thirty-five dollars which they divided among them. "If our men keep on encountering the enemy," said one, "we will get a sufficiency of the most approved arms at but little cost since, after making a show, they will abandon their dead and run for their lives." A Richmond reporter observed that the Northern journals groaned in the most dismal tones over the result of the Bethel battle. "The inordinate love of life among the invaders is the most obvious explanation," he commented. "The victory is one of the most extraordinary in the annals of war! Four thousand thoroughly drilled and

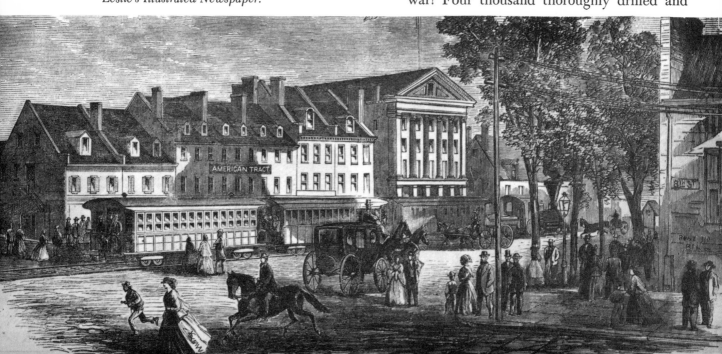

Cavalry charge in Virginia. *Harper's Weekly.*

equipped troops routed and driven from the field by only eleven hundred men! Two hundred of the enemy killed, and on our side but one life lost [Private Henry L. Wyatt]. Does not the hand of God seem manifest in this war? From the attack upon Fort Sumter to the present moment the preservation of Southern life amidst such murderous assaults as have been made by the enemy, seems little less than miraculous.

"The courage and conduct of the noble sons of the South engaged in this battle are beyond all praise. They have crowned the name of their country with imperishable luster, and made their own names immortal. They have achieved a complete victory, putting their enemies to inglorious flight, and given the world a brilliant pledge of the manner in which the South can defend its firesides and altars. The North has always won its battles on paper—the South is content to achieve hers

The first Market-house, one of the busiest corners in Richmond. *Frank Leslie's Illustrated Newspaper.*

The Exchange Hotel, in the right wing of which the Richmond Post Office was located, was surrounded by a rowdy neighborhood. *Valentine Museum.*

in the field. Let us invoke our heroic soldiers not to permit this splendid success in any way to relax their vigilance and their energy. Let them be as prudent as they are brave, as vigilant as they are determined, and all is secure. Let them omit no preparation, no watchfulness, no precaution which the presence of the bravest enemy might require—in other words, let them always trust in God and keep their powder dry, and our soil will soon be delivered from the boastful braggarts who have dared to pollute it."

Local matters were now taking a turn for the worse. "No business here!" shouted the merchants. "Owing to the impossibility of procuring supplies except for cash, sales hereafter will be for cash!" Richmond was beginning to feel the first pinch of the Federal blockade of its Southern ports, and of the percenters and extortionists of the future. Another army was moving into the city and the people were finding themselves surrounded by a variety of shady characters. Graft and shoddy deals were the order of the day. This added to the duties of the Mayor, the police, and other city officials. Prices were booming, and an effort was made to nip small-time war profiteering before it got out of hand. City ordinances were passed for this purpose but, as usual, offenders paid no attention to such measures. Hence the little band of per-centers grew into battalions of high-bracket extortioners within a short time. One of the first examples was the case of two men who bought all the chickens in the First Market and sold them the same day for a much higher price (an infringement of a city ordinance), for which they were heavily fined. Violations of other city ordinances were increasing and the offenders were crowding the Mayor's Court. On one day alone, his calendar listed some thirty cases of which these are representative: Catherine Garibaldi, who claimed no kin with the Emperor hero, was fined five dollars for selling "blue rain" without a license, and five dollars more for keeping her barroom open after 10 P.M. Many others were fined the same amount for the same offense, some having kept open on the preceding Sunday. Ruben Gillen was fined ten dollars for permitting Negroes to assemble unlawfully at his house, and a number of hack drivers were fined half that amount for operating unlicensed vehicles. Another was cautioned about the ordinance barring Negroes from being taught to read.

Meanwhile, the police were on the double with other local matters. Houses in the rear of the Exchange Hotel, occupied by parties of dubious and uncertain character, were a prolific source of many disgraceful rows which the police had been called upon to quell. It was said that the houses "contained many nests of vile and unclean birds." People who had occasion to walk by the locality saw that the occupants themselves had well-grounded apprehension of the dangers which beset them, having boarded up all their accessible doors and windows, thus preparing for miniature bombardments. One resident had been arrested for chasing a neighbor down the street with a saber; another for "performing sundry movements in a passage of that popular establishment [the Exchange Hotel] while not fully clothed." Still another was "placed in limbo for an exhibition of pugnacity in the alley way." A. J. Ford, proprietor of a drinking saloon in that neighborhood, was summoned before His Honor to show cause why he should not be fined for keeping his establishment open after 10 P.M., contrary to the city ordinance. Ford said his place had been broken open by "a parcel of men" who helped themselves to anything they pleased, and that he had been perfectly powerless to do anything about it. They had previously gone to the nearby "Cyprian's Retreat" kept by Miss Clara Coleman, smashed all the furniture, and had done similar "naughty tricks" in that region the same night. Ford was fined and dismissed.

Henry McQuire, James Christian, and John Morrison were arrested by the night watch for "allowing their hides to get full of corn juice, the article being the basis for an attack made by them on a warehouse where they pounded the watchman, John Doerflinger, on the head with a slugshot for interfering with their amusement. Considerable noise and confusion prevailed during the *muss*, and there was evidence of a general tendency to disorder." Bail was put up for their good behavior.

A beetle-browed individual named Ben Read was carried before the Mayor for feloniously cutting, stabbing, and wounding William J. Somerville with intent to maim, disable, disfigure, and kill him. Somerville first struck Read a blow with his fist, which the latter returned "by ripping open his bowels with a knife and making some ugly gashes about his shoulder." At this juncture, Somerville fell from loss of blood, and the watchmen, making their appearance, carried Read to the lockup. A woman was at the bottom of the whole difficulty; "a little piece of feminine mischief, called Mrs. Evans, was fancied by both parties," read the report. "Read had been the longest 'lover,' Somerville months since. The latter feared Read would get the inside track of him and tried to scare him off, with the result above related. The woman who caused the *muss* fondled around the prisoner [Read] like a sick kitten to a pan of milk. She is, however, another man's wife, and we should judge a rather poor specimen of constancy. Read was commuted for examination — if Somerville, the ex-Custom House robber, doesn't die in the meantime."

Mrs. Giovanni Deveto was summoned before the Mayor for cowhiding Juan Luce in the street. The complainant testified that she had performed the operation in a most powerful and convincing manner, and proposed to show evidence which was declined by the Mayor. It appeared that the dispute between them had arisen about the ownership of some barrels of tobacco, during which Luce had called Mrs. Deveto some outrageous names and applied an epithet to her, which she answered by applying a cowskin. The Mayor said he would not approve of the acts of the parties; it certainly was not right for the woman to use the weapon or for the man to provoke her to do it. The account being about equally balanced, he dismissed the case, leaving the ownership of the tobacco to be determined at a later date.

Sometimes the whites and blacks stirred up trouble between themselves. Mary Grimes, a free woman of color, was arrested on a warrant of Ida Wilson who charged her with calling her bad names and retaining forty dollars' worth of clothing. The complainant was one of that class who had a great deal of washing to send out and who, as some of her sisters had done before her, found it inconvenient to foot the bill. Ida Wilson owed the Negro for the washing and the Negro got it upon returning Ida's clothes.

But all was not rough and tumble in the City of the Seven Hills. Midsummer 1861 had arrived and reporters were writing, "We never saw the streets more populous with human beings. Men, women, children, and soldiers are on the move continually. A gentle breeze prevails, while overhead the fleeting clouds are so commingled that they act as a fine barrier to keep out the too ardent gaze of the impassioned 'Old Sol.' " The celebrated battalion of the New Orleans Washington Artillery had arrived, numbering four companies and three hundred men, "the pride of the Crescent City, its members being both soldiers and gentlemen." It possessed eight splendid brass field-pieces and rifle cannon, and was otherwise well armed. One hundred and twenty horses were required to draw the guns and other equipment. In their visit to Capitol Square, they marched around the Washington monument, each man with uncovered head, and saluted the statue of the first President with becoming reverence. The large number of spectators seemed to sympathize with the motive and the act, for everyone was silent, "as if invoking the spirit of the mighty dead to look upon and encourage those who now strive to emulate his deeds," reported the press. "It was really an interesting scene in which U. S. General Winfield Scott, who was present at the inauguration of the statue, might have been proud to have participated."

Acts of heroism were beginning to be eulogized in the Richmond newspapers. One townsman, Captain O. Jennings Wise of the Blues, had performed an act of gallantry at the recent fight at Acquia Creek which his friends thought deserved to be immortalized in history. While the cannonading between the shore battery and the ships was at its height, the fearless young commander stood outside the parapet, where the bullets were raining hottest, exposing his own person to their deadly effects, that he might give timely warning to his men so they could avoid the danger. "How does every pulse thrill, and the heart swell with grateful emotions as we contemplate such scenes of similar heroes which we have in our armies," noted a reporter, "ready to peril all for the just cause, and sacrifice everything rather than submit to degradation and dishonor."

Influenced by such eulogies and the tramp of marching feet, little boys became "out-and-out military men." Marbles, tops, hoops, kites, and books were put aside. Youngsters no longer went to bed dreaming of the fun they were to have the next day in a game of ball or knock-up-and-span. Their night visions were made up of juvenile squads to drill, of youthful companies, battalions, regiments, armies— all on the move to meet a foe. They awakened to buckle on a harmless sword and collect schoolmates into line. On the streets they wore the jaunty army fatigue cap, pants with

A cartoon which asks: "Do not the long skirts kindle a Christian feeling in our hearts when leaving church?" *Harper's Weekly*.

a stripe down each side, and saluted *à la militaire*. As they looked around the well-filled benches of the schoolroom, their eyes were of the soldier and their thoughts "What a show we would make if we were all mustered into the army." Their dimes were carefully saved to buy toy swords. Their recruiting office was anywhere and everywhere, and long lines of little boys were to be seen drilling in every street. They ignored with supreme contempt the confectionery, and passed with military hauteur the toy shops—except those which displayed some frail representative article of warfare. "They build, assault, and capture a half dozen Fort Sumters every day, and devise all sorts of schemes to prevent their reinforcements," said the press. "Such are the little boys of the present day, and they generally make the right sort of men." Within a short time, the little boys were giving the police and civic authorities plenty of trouble.

The Reverend D. S. Doggett, D. D., preached an eloquent and able sermon one Sunday in the Broad Street Methodist Episcopal Church, his subject "the present crusade against our liberties." He did not advise his brethren or friends to stand idly by; quite the reverse. If the Confederate cause was not a good one, could it recommend itself to the ap-

proval of the pure and good, both religious and otherwise, of all classes, kinds, and conditions of society? He thought not. The general complaint of a great lack of church attendance by young men in Richmond was answered by the statement that their many and varied services with the military prevented their presence at such a time. One reporter gave his personal reasons which were detailed and ample in every respect:

"Non-Churchgoers' Excuses. — Overslept myself; could not dress in time; too windy; too dusty; too wet; too damp; too sunny; too cloudy; don't feel disposed; no other time to myself; look over my drawers; put my papers to rights; letters to write to friends; mean to take a ride; tied to business six days in a week; no fresh air but on Sunday; can't breathe in church; always so full; feel a little feverish; feel a little chilly; feel very lazy; expect company to dinner; got a headache; intend nursing myself today; new bonnet not come home; tore my muslin dress down stairs; got a new novel, must be returned on Monday morning; wasn't shaved in time; don't like the liturgy—always praying for the same thing; don't like extemporary prayers; don't like an organ—'tis too noisy; don't like singing without music—makes me nervous; the spirit is willing but the

The Monumental Church, Richmond. *Library of of Congress.*

flesh is weak; dislike an extemporaneous service—it is too frothy; can't bear a written sermon—too prosy; nobody today but our own minister; can't always listen to the same preacher; don't like strangers; can't keep awake when I'm at church—fell asleep last time I was there—don't mean to risk it again; mean to inquire of sensible persons about the propriety of going to such a place as church, and publish the result."

Several companies of the Virginia militia were holding public musters, the officers in command being determined to get their men ready in case their services were demanded. At the time, however, the military spirit was so high that it was doubtful it would ever be necessary to resort to the drafting process. When it was known that such a course was essential to the preservation of the public liberties, the authorities contended that all the militia would come forward and volunteer to drive back the enemy from Virginia soil. Most of the militia would prove to be anything but raw recruits, for they knew how to handle a gun, and, banded together in regiments, they would not run from any enemy.

A proclamation issued by the Honorable John Letcher, the Governor of Virginia, made it official that the State did not contemplate the drafting of the militia for the present war, but it did make an eloquent appeal to every patriotic and loyal Virginian within the borders of the Old Dominion to be actively engaged in its defense. He called for all volunteer companies, not already mustered into state service, to go forthwith to the places designated and be mustered in. He invoked the good people of Virginia to organize themselves speedily into other volunteer companies, and, taking such arms as they had or might be able to procure, to march to such places of rendezvous. He required the Militia of the Line to hold themselves in readiness for immediate service, and to drill under their officers at least once a week. Furthermore, he enjoined all to deport themselves with the calmness and composure becoming the people of a great Commonwealth conscious of their rights, and resolved to maintain them, never doubting that, by devotion, energy, and determination, the liberty, independence, and integrity, the safety, honor, and welfare of the Confederate States would be supported and sustained.

The Governor's request was answered by a flood of notices in the press: "HDQRS. RICHMOND ZOUAVES, Corinthian Hall. ALL MEMBERS OF THIS COMPANY are hereby ordered to attend drill every night at half-past 8 o'clock from this date. All persons disposed to enter the service of the State will call promptly and enroll their names, as the corps will go into service immediately. Uniforms and equipment furnished free. By order of E. McConnell. John Regan, O.S."

"To Volunteers—I propose to form a Volunteer Artillery Company of good material, for the period required by law. Best guns, uniforms, tents, including all things necessary for the most efficient and comfortable service, will be had. John Howard."

"SPECIAL NOTICE. EVERY MAN IN VIRGINIA, capable of Military service, should now be a member of some military organization, and ready to take the field. It is proposed to form a company of infantry to volunteer for active service. All persons wishing to join such a company are requested to leave their names with the undersigned, at the office of the Virginia Life Insurance Company, at the corner of Main and 11th streets. Roscoe E. Heath."

"Attention Bloody Run Guard—All who have joined this company, and all who wish to join, will meet at Company G's Hall, Church Hill, on Wednesday evening. Come all, as *this is the Company*. The Committee."

The Jackson Guards were ready to muster twenty-five additional men into service, and many other such military groups were calling for recruits. Among the troops with full quotas were the scalping Texas Rangers, encamped at Howard's Grove. They were soon to leave for the Northwest, their equipment including bowie knives "to strike terror in the soul of all Lincolnites. They ask no quarter and give none." The Fifth Louisiana Regiment of Volunteers, under Colonel Hunt, one thousand strong, with twenty railroad cars to accommodate them, were loading their baggage for Yorktown.

Women too were joining in the war services. The ladies of the Centenary Church were there every day from early morning until late evening, making up articles needed by the troops. The ladies of the Leigh Street Baptist Church announced they were ready and willing to do all they could in making clothing for soldiers. "Capt. Z. S. Magruder, of the Henri Company Dragoons, recognized the reception of 50 pairs of Drawers from the Book Aid Society, for which, in his own name, and in the name and on the part of his company, he begs leave to return his sincere thanks and heartfelt gratitude," read an acknowledgment in the press. The Ladies' Soldiers' Aid Society of St. Paul's Episcopal Church was collecting a variety of items which could be used by the men in service. They, in common with the congregations of other churches and organizations located elsewhere, demonstrated their faith in the government and the army by their works.

"If anybody doubts our ladies are not patriotic and self-sacrificing, let him protrude himself into the large empty store under the Spotswood Hotel any time during the day or evening," wrote an observer, "and he will see a sight that will make his heart beat a tattoo against his masculine ribs. About thirty of the prettiest young ladies in Richmond, attached to the Monumental Episcopal Church, are there engaged in the manufacture of shirts, pantaloons, havelocks, and other garments necessary to the comfort of our brave volunteers, forming as sweet a bouquet of loveliness and patriotism as was ever gathered from the garden of Nature. It makes a man's heart go 'thump-a-te-thump' against his stomach just to go by the door. For young soldiers there is a sign: 'NO ADMITTANCE EXCEPT ON BUSINESS.' Old fellows will please keep on the other side of the street. There is not a flower in the flock who doesn't deserve the sweetest kind of an e-osp-se-weeptee-e-e-e indefinitely drawn out. P.S. For the benefit of the uninitiated, we would observe that the above is the Hottentot for 'kiss.'"

To aid in these efforts, many stores in Richmond agreed to close at an earlier hour each evening so that young men employees would be free to drill and the young women could devote the extra time to the work of supplying needed articles for the men in the service.

Since the establishment of the hospital on Twenty-sixth Street, the ladies and gentlemen of that neighborhood had been untiring in their efforts to see that invalids there wanted for nothing that kindness could suggest or that money could buy. This was given as an instance where a few patriots located near hospitals had the burden of care and attention thrust upon them while others in distant parts of the city contributed little or nothing to the welfare of sick and wounded soldiers. "We feel sure that it will not be necessary to mention this matter in connection with neighborhoods where such attention is needed," hinted one reporter. "Our soldiers fight for all of us, so let all of us do our duty to them wherever we live." Many other "noble people" of Richmond were taking sick and wounded soldiers to their homes for care and treatment.

The rains came often to Richmond during the summer, "heavy and fast for an hour or more, to the perfect disgruntlement of the dust but the delight of the people and young ducks." For a few days, at least, the streets were clean as a new penny and rendered unnecessary the use of the inevitable dust eradicator, the Niagara watering machine. The Fourth of July brought clear weather. Con-

Professor Lowe at his aerial lookout post. Confederates called him "The Professor of Gas." *National Archives.*

federate flags and banners streamed in the breeze, sidewalks were filled with beautiful ladies, young soldiers, and older inhabitants; the streets with prancing horses, buggies, carts, army wagons—"distributed here and there to make up the mass of our city life refreshing to behold." Most of the theaters were closed, but horseracing and band concerts were drawing crowds and affording entertainment suitable to the season. The pleasant shade of the numerous trees on Capitol Square was sought by soldiers and visitors to the city as well as residents.

"We begin to feel as if we were really the metropolis of the South," crowed a reporter. "We have visitors by the thousands who meet us at every step, and we almost forget the quaint, staid days of 'Auld Lang Syne,' when every countenance was as familiar as the curbstones, and we felt like one family. Whatever may have been the drawbacks of the war, in some respects it has certainly given Richmond a start and a pace which she never knew before. We hope it will be kept up until we are the Queen City of the South. If the Old Baboon [Lincoln] could see our streets and parks thronged with so many cheerful faces and groups of soldiers lounging and laughing everywhere, he would think he had not made much progress in subjugating us."

A partial answer from the "Old Baboon" came one afternoon when a balloon was seen passing over the city, and the same reporter noted "It may have been the notorious 'Professor Lowe,' one of the Ape's aerial corps enlisted to aid in 'subduing the South.' If so, we advise the people, wherever he touches *terra firma,* to give him something to remember them by. As a spy, by the rules of war, he deserves death. He once started from Cincinnati and landed in South Carolina. Balloons are given to the enactment of strange feats. If it were the 'professor,' let him be treated accordingly—and not in the easiest way either." Lowe was the first to use a balloon for observing movements of enemy troops, and his experiments became well known during the War between the States.

But when the weather was hot, *it was hot!* Reporters mentioned the approaching dog days with shudders having nothing to do with a chill. "The sun, for the week past, has been pouring down his vertical rays at a forty horsepower rate on the denizens of this promising city," one complained. "This is a fact, the existence of which no one hereabouts questions, unless he resides in the ice-house. People, male and female, who are not compelled by the calls of business, select the 'early morn' or 'dewy eve' for those pedal exercises which give roses to the cheek and health to the body. If they did not, one or two days' hearty exercise, as things go now, would result in a residuum no larger than a grease spot. As Bailey's Festus says, 'it is no task for suns to shine.' If it were, they would not indulge the practice to the extent they do in such alarmingly hot times. 'Center of light and energy! Thy way is through the unknown void,' but we can spare some of your surplus effulgence. Go to Old Point Comfort. The Yankees will welcome you!" Since it was becoming so hot that Southerners could hardly bear it, the reporter wondered if the Yankees at Old Point Comfort were very *comfortable* and enjoying

The incessant cries of hucksters during the summer brought complaints from Richmond residents. Drawing by W. L. Sheppard for *Every Saturday*, an illustrated weekly.

Professor Thaddeus S. C. Lowe, the eminent and troublesome Yankee balloonist. *National Archives.*

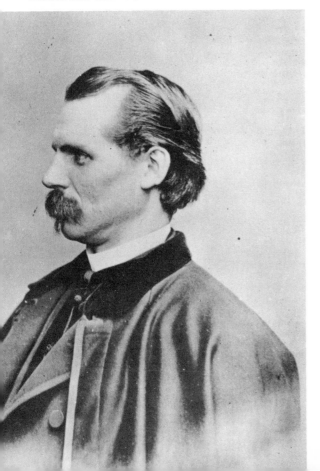

excellent health. "Let them wait until July and August when the heat is really 'cumulative'!" he mused.

Fruits were ripe, and everywhere the people of Richmond were hearing the cries of the hucksters. Pineapples, at prices slightly above the usual cost, and other tropical imports were not so plentiful as formerly but still available. Their arrival, "thanks to our bold privateers running the blockade," was reported as "an agreeable incident." Home-grown fruits were abundant, especially watermelons, which were peddled on a door-to-door basis with shrieking voices announcing several other items for sale. "Though not in favor of abridging the liberty of speech," observed an editor, "it would relieve the public of an annoyance if the usual yelling could be dispensed with.

"Plagued with more than one war (watermelon), if anybody deserves choking it is that class of pug-nosed, dirty-faced, high-flavored, ragged, lean, bony class of animated skeletons who ride lazily through our streets crying charcoal and fruit. They send forth sounds

57

In summer everyone wanted to live in "the ice house." *Valentine Museum.*

that harrow up a man's soul, especially when writing an editorial, and make one say things internally which outwardly would give him a bad character for eloquence. To all such noisy demonstrations we say 'if you must be endured, keep your mouth shut under our windows—dry up, evaporate, leave us as rapidly as possible.' To our own Mayor we present them as a 'crying evil,' and respectfully ask for their suspension."

Since the paper mills of the city had warned that the supply of their product was becoming limited, newspapers carried many pleas such as this one: "RAGS WANTED—In these pitying times paper is a desideratum. Let the people therefore save all the rags which will be wanted by the paper mill, and can be disposed of readily at fair prices."

More important to the government, however, was the manufacture of war matériel, especially cannon. No greater fortune could

The Commissary Storehouses near the canal. *National Archives.*

have been bequeathed the Confederacy by the powers in Washington than the resources it had once used in the immediate vicinity of Richmond itself. The requisites for such a project were iron, coal, water power, and facilities of transportation, and the Southern Capital had all of these in abundance. The quality of the James River iron was known to be the finest in America, and twelve miles distant there was an inexhaustible supply of coal. The United States Government had fully understood the unequaled advantages of Richmond in this respect, and a large proportion of the cannon for the Federal army and navy had been made there. Experience had demonstrated that local shops had turned out the best cannon in the country, and probably in the world.

The Kanawha canal supplied an amount of water power equivalent to that of any other city in the United States. The boats following its course brought iron and coal to the factories and carried the manufactured products to the adjoining river, or any other point along the way, for transshipment. In addition to these advantages, Richmond had an unusual number of large iron foundries employing a vast mechanical force which, in an emergency, made them independent of aid from other sources. One of these was the Tredegar Iron Works, which had constructed the machinery of the largest frigates in the United States navy and now was devoting all its efforts to the manufacture of cannon and other war essentials for the Confederate Government. The smaller concerns also joined in the undertaking; without this combination of resources it would have been almost impossible for the South to have carried on the war.

The city was rife with rumors about events in the neighborhood of Manassas Junction. The defeat of Confederate outposts at Philippi, West Virginia, by General George B. McClellan had been balanced by the defeat of a Union reconnaissance at Vienna, Virginia, only to shift once more in favor of the Yankees at Rich Mountain, where McClellan popped up again to win another victory.

While the people of Richmond were asking, "What next?" a reporter wrote an imaginary

"The Bend," looking down the James River from Richmond. *National Archives.*

The Tredegar Iron Works, in which many of the cannon used by Confederate gunners were cast. *Library of Congress.*

account of a conversation between Lincoln and General Winfield Scott. They were described as seated together during a review of troops in the Federal Capital, and, as thousands of Yankees marched by them, "the gouty old general told the King of the Abolitionists a most unpalatable truth. 'General,' said the King, 'this is a splendid army and costs the Government a heap of money daily; but why is it remaining here idle? You once penetrated to the Capital of Mexico in three months with only one-fifth of the force you have now. Why do you not push on into Virginia and take possession of the Capital of the rebellious Old Dominion?' Said the General, 'The reason is plain and palpable. The men who carried me to the city of Mexico are the same who are now keeping me out of Virginia.'"

More serious was the order issued by Confederate General John B. Magruder, commanding an area including Richmond, which was published at this time. It directed all officers and soldiers to restrain from reporting army movements, results of battles and skirmishes, the number of forces at particular points, and all other information favorable to the enemy. Taking the hint, the Richmond press retorted:

"Neither the Generals, nor the Department, nor anybody that has any right to know, is in the habit of communicating with us, touching secrets connected with the war. That such secrets have sometimes leaked out, is probably true, but that they have been divulged through our aid and connivance, is not the fact. As a general rule, the press of a country ought to abstain from publishing any intelligence which can give information to the enemy. In the beginning of hostilities, it is obvious that journalists, unaccustomed to a state of war, may err in this respect. Our own Southern press, at the outset, announced the arrival and departure of regiments from particular points, and other matters of general notoriety, which, no doubt, the enemy was fully apprised of by his numerous allies and spies within our own borders; but the practice has been judiciously given up, much to the secret disgruntlement of many, whose curi-

osity desired the information, and yet who, with charming inconsistency, berated the newspapers roundly for publishing military movements. Even when people have something to do, faultfinding is a luxury which they manage to make time for; and when they have nothing to do, it is their sole occupation."

The provisional Confederate Congress met and passed a law providing for the election of a President, Vice-President, and members of Congress—under a permanent Constitution—to be held on the first Wednesday in November. Electors of the President and Vice-President were to meet in their respective states and cast votes on the first Wednesday in December. Congress was to assemble on February 18, 1862, and the inauguration of the President was to be held on the twenty-second day of that month.

In his message to the Congress, President Davis said: "I deemed it advisable to direct the removal of the several Executive Departments, with their archives to this city, to which you have removed the seat of Government, immediately after your adjournment. The aggressive movements of the enemy required prompt and energetic action. This accumulation of his forces on the Potomac sufficiently demonstrated that his efforts were to be directed against Virginia; and from no point could the necessary measures for her defense and protection be so efficiently directed as from her own capital."

He had no sooner delivered his message than the cannons were booming on the battlefield of Bull Run at Manassas. He left Richmond immediately and arrived in time to take part in the battle. The heaviest onslaught of the enemy was made on the Confederate left under General Joseph E. Johnston, and it was that division which suffered the greatest loss. It continued to be pressed during the whole day, until about four o'clock in the afternoon, when President Davis advanced his center, disengaged a portion of the enemy's forces, and "decided the fortune of the day."

The Richmond press responded in boldface headlines: TERRIFIC BATTLE! OUR ARMY AGAIN VICTORIOUS!! GREAT SLAUGHTER ON BOTH SIDES.

The Stone Bridge, near Manassas, Virginia. *National Archives.*

BEAUREGARD'S HORSE SHOT FROM UNDER HIM! GENERAL MCDOWELL WOUNDED! THE ENEMY IN FULL RETREAT! "Manassas Junction, July 21— A battle, lasting ten hours, was fought at Stone Bridge today. We have the inexpressible satisfaction of announcing another victory of our arms, a decisive victory after the most hotly contested and most important battle ever fought on the American continent. The numbers engaged on each side were far beyond precedent in American history; and, fought as the battle was, under the gaze of two Capitals of two powerful Confederacies, it possessed an interest and significance such as has attached to few battles ever fought before.

"General G. T. Beauregard had a miraculous escape from death when his horse was shot from under him while leading Hampton's Legion into action. General Johnston seized the colors of a wavering regiment and rallied them to the charge. We have not been able to estimate the number of dead and wounded. It is reported that the Federal commander, General Irvin McDowell, was wounded. On our side, General Francis Bartow, of Georgia, is dead. President Davis arrived on the battlefield after the action had commenced."

It was there that Brigadier General Thomas J. Jackson got his famous "Stonewall" sobriquet. In the heat of the battle, Brigadier General Barnard E. Bee, rallying his Confederate troops, pointed to Jackson and cried, "There is General Jackson standing like a stone wall. Let us determine to die here, and we will conquer. Follow me!" Within an hour, General Bee was dead. A Richmond war correspondent, also in the heat of the battle, wrote:

"Altogether it was the most decided downright whipping the Yankees ever received on Virginia soil. They had the advantage of ground and the advantage of numbers. We

Ruins of the Stone Bridge after the Battle of Bull Run. *National Archives.*

The Battle of Bull Run, July 21, 1861. *Frank Leslie's Illustrated Newspaper.*

had men enough, but never had more than 1,200 men in the field at one time, while they were leading 15,000 men on at one charge. Their famous Sherman battery did not intimidate us in the least, and we had the pleasure to send today two of their most splendid rifle cannon to Manassas. I believe we got muskets enough to equip a good-sized battalion, and there is no end to the haversacks and canteens which they threw away in their flight. Amongst other things, our wagons brought us today a load of caps and hats, which shows that, after all, the Yankees must have a great respect for us, or they would not have taken them off for us. Well, at 7 o'clock P.M. we stopped firing, but they did not stop retreating, and there the fun ended for the day."

Reports that the Yankees had handcuffs, chains, and halters among their equipment for hanging rebels (which Federal officers denied) prompted the press to exclaim, "For what and for whom! It is easy to guess. To treat as guilty felons, to enslave and secure for a felon's death, the patriotic sons of the South, whose only crime is the defense of constitutional liberty, and resistance to the usurper and tyrant at Washington."

During the battle of Bull Run, a Mississippi soldier, Brigadier Quartermaster Pryor, was taken prisoner by Private Hasbrouck of the Wisconsin Second Regiment. Captured by accident as he rode his horse into the Federal lines, Pryor discovered his mistake when he said to Hasbrouck, "We are getting badly cut to pieces." Hasbrouck asked, "What regiment do you belong to?" and Pryor answered, "The Nineteenth Mississippi." Hasbrouck drew his pistol and said, "Then you are my prisoner." Pryor described an officer, "the most prominent in the fight, distinguished from the rest by his white horse," as Jeff Davis. He also confirmed reports of a regiment of Negro troops in the Confederate forces. He said it was difficult to get them "in proper discipline and battle array." Among the prisoners captured by the Confederates was one of Ellsworth's wounded Zouaves. He confessed that, when the Yankees left Washington, he was assured he would dine in Richmond that week. "You're here, ain't you?" said a rebel

Rallying the troops of Bee, Bartow, and Evans, behind the Robinson house at the Battle of Bull Run. *National Park Service*.

Retreat of Federal troops during the onslaught of Confederate forces at Bull Run. *Library of Congress*.

soldier. "I sure am," answered the Zouave, "but how the hell am I going to eat with a ball [bullet] in my belly?"

Another Confederate soldier, who had also been in the fight at Bull Run, said that the Yankees had sought to gain a mean advantage over them by advancing with "the glorious flag of the Confederacy" instead of their own Stars and Stripes. Believing them to be their own men, they were almost surrounded before they realized that Yankees were upon them and opened fire. This was not substantiated in any military dispatch or report by Confederate officers. What really occurred had been seen by General Beauregard himself, and he determined that it never would happen again. On the battlefield he had noted that the Confederate flag, with its Stars and Bars, when seen through haze or dust, might be mistaken for the Stars and Stripes and thus endanger the Confederate forces. Hence, other designs were made up and used at various times during the war. The most popular was known as the Battle Flag.

The President, while at Manassas Junction, raised Beauregard from the rank of Brigadier to the rank of full General in token of his achievements at Bull Run. Since Lee had organized the Virginia troops and put them in the field, thereby contributing importantly to the success of the army under Johnston and Beauregard, why was Lee not there at the time Davis, on his white horse, and other generals were gathering military laurels with Lee's own troops? No satisfactory answer ever has been given, but the possibility that Davis was keeping Lee in the background—even that he was jealous of the General's popularity—has received credence. From Richmond, Lee wrote to his wife: "I wished to partake in the struggle, and am mortified at my absence. But the President thought it more important that I should be here. I could not have done as well as has been done, but I could have helped and taken part in a struggle for my home and neighborhood. So the work is done, I care not by whom it is done. I leave tomorrow for the army in Western Virginia."

Firing a salute of one hundred guns at the Capitol in Richmond after news of the Confederate victory at Bull Run. From a sketch by an officer of the Confederate army. *Frank Leslie's Illustrated Newspaper*.

A camp of Confederate soldiers hidden from Yankee observers in the pocket of a hill. *National Archives.*

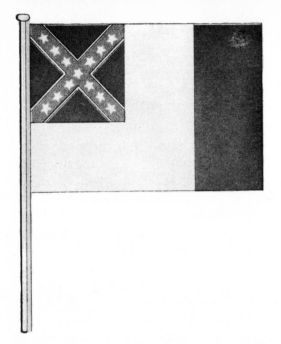

A Short, Sharp War

Another day of fasting and prayer, designated by the President for "returning thanks to the Most High in giving us victory in the late battle" was observed throughout the city. The solemn occasion had scarcely ended before the Richmond press put on its spurs, defied and damned the Yankees, and cried out for recognition of the Confederacy:

"The Northern Congressmen and journals redouble their menaces of death and destruction to the South. The South scorns and defies them. They don't know the people they are dealing with. They can never overrun this country. Their threats to violate women, to despoil farms, to make us their vassals, would convert even a nation of cowards into a nation of heroes. What, then, must be its effect upon a race as heroic as ever lived in all the tide of time? Nor do they misconstrue the calm contempt of the South for the foolish boastings of their vulgar Congressmen, and its forbearance to prisoners as the result of fear or a desire to propitiate them. The answer of the South to their brutal slang is in her sword—such an answer as they received at Bethel Church, at Bull Run, and at Manassas. Let them multiply their forces. We shall have as many men in the field as themselves, and that will be twice as many as we shall need. Let them go on with their threats to hang Jeff Davis and his Cabinet. When they begin their hanging game on the humblest son of the South that breathes, the best life they have shall pay for it, and if Lincoln and his Cabi-net are not swung from one scaffold, it will be because they have concluded to conduct the war with humanity, or have escaped from Washington in Scotch caps, long cloaks, and fast midnight trains. In his Message to Congress, Old Abe said that 'so large an army as the Government has now on foot was never before known.' It is clear that he does not read his Bible, for the books of Exodus and Numbers inform us that the Israelites had an army of 603,350, and all volunteers at that.

"Now, Harriet Beecher Stowe proposes that the present struggle between the North and the South shall be designated The Religious War. In this we are inclined to agree with the author of *Uncle Tom's Cabin*. It is a religious war. It is the Bible and a pure Christianity against infidelity and God-dishonoring crimes, and we are glad to see that the Churches of the South are alive to their responsibility in this regard. We learn that in two days during the present week 176,000 pages of religious tracts were sent from this city to the various encampments.

"The Washington dispatches contain a rumor that General Wood has superseded Butler in the command at Fortress Monroe. The civilian Generals are evidently feeling the guillotine. Heretofore the complaint has been that they had plenty of men but no officers; and we apprehend that by the time they get the officers they will have no men. Old 'Fuss and Feathers' [General Winfield Scott] has been placed in the background,

~~P~~RISONERS LET LOOSE IN GEORGIA —On Mon-
~~y~~ last (says the Harris County Enterprise), du~~~~
~~g~~ the presence of a large number of persons
~~m~~ the country in our village, three prisoners
~~re~~ rescued from the hands of the officers, by
~~several~~ persons in disguise. They had been ar-
~~rested~~, and, waiving a preliminary examination,
~~d~~ asked for time to make bond. Before the
~~me~~ allowed them had expired, they were res-
~~ued~~ and had disappeared.

CAPTURED.—On Monday last, near Conrad's
~~St~~ore, Rockingham county, seven runaway negroes
~~we~~re captured. Six of them were taken by Major
~~G~~en. W. Miller, and one by his brother. They
~~w~~ere a part of a gang of thirty or thirty-two who
~~h~~ad all started at one time.

☞ Some of President Jeff Davis's admirers in
Rome, Ga., are making preparations to present
him a fine buggy. Such a present to him seems
entirely unnecessary. We guess he will soon
find the official bed he sleeps in a little buggy.—
Prentice.

ROBBING MAILS IN ALABAMA.—The mail was
robbed at Lafayette, Chambers county, Ala., on
last Monday night. Amount stolen unknown.

Newspaper dispatches from the Federal Capital often
included quips aimed at Jefferson Davis such as the
one above in the Washington, D. C., *Evening Star.*

and General McClellan takes his place in the
front of the picture. This is apparent from the
Washington dispatches. General McClellan
does this, and General McClellan does that,
but not one word of the veteran Dr. Scott.
Nobody pities the defunct Chieftain—no one
does him reverence.

"The favorite epithet with the Yankees is
rebels, a term implying a right on their part
to govern, and the duty on ours of obedience.
They have convinced themselves that we are
an inferior sort of people; that it is they who
support, feed, and protect us; that we are
under the ban of mankind and the frown of
Heaven, for the sin of slavery, and that it is by
virtue of their own extraordinary righteous-
ness and favor in the sight of the Almighty,
and of the countenance and protection which
they choose to vouchsafe unto us, that Heaven
mitigates its frowns, Earth mollifies its anger,
and we are permitted to exist.

"That we, therefore, poor, helpless and
weak, should presume to 'secede' from their
patronizing alliance; that we should attempt

to shuffle off what they consider the 'mortal
coil,' refusing life and committing flat suicide
by the separation, strikes them with amazement and indignation. They consider they are
doing a most righteous thing by preserving us
in their holy keeping, and, by running away,
we deprive them of the luxury of an ostenta-
tious and most profitable charity.

"Unless we are helpless, imbecile, pauper,
heathen, revolting from a guardianship of
godliness and benevolence deserving of infi-
nite gratitude, their epithet, rebels, applied to
us is really as honorable as it was in the case
of the fathers of the country in the Revolution. Then, no less a man than the great Fox,
annoyed at the flippant use of the term by the
minions of government in parliament, rebuked
them by declaring: 'The term rebel is no certain mark of disgrace. All the great asserters
of liberty, the saviors of their country, the
benefactors of mankind in all ages, have been
called rebels. We owe the Constitution which
enables us to sit in this house to a rebellion!'

"A short, sharp war was the favorite plan
for the subjugation of the South. The interests
of Northern commerce would not permit the
war to be long, and, therefore, they insisted
that Richmond and Memphis must be occupied in July, and the 22nd of February
succeeding be celebrated by the invaders in
New Orleans. This was no doubt a convenient
arrangement for the commercial interests, but
Manassas has interposed an insuperable ob-
stacle to the execution of that program.

"The battle of the 21st has decided the
question of recognition. The complete overthrow of the flower of the Northern army; the
capture of a number of guns unprecedented
in the history of warfare, with immense army
stores and munitions; the utter rout and dismay of the enemy; the threatening of the
Northern Capital; the panic of its inhabitants
and of the Government, to be soon followed
by their flight from the city, are facts which
must extort from the rulers of the earth a
recognition of our power and capacity for national self-existence.

"The enemy's Congress had confessed that
the Southern movements vastly exceeded the
proportions of a rebellion, by granting half a

million of men and five hundred millions of dollars for the war of subjugation. Eleven sovereign States were in league in the movement. All the insignia and organism of a distinct and independent national existence were visible. Of every attribute and function of nationality the Confederacy were in possession. There was but one thing wanting to recognition, and that was a demonstration that we were able in fact to make good our resistance to the North in its effort to compel us back into the Union. Nations may be ever so well disposed toward a struggling nationality. They may desire to recognize its existence as distinct and independent. They may be anxious to establish relations of friendship and intercourse with it; but they would commit themselves awkwardly if they recognized a Government that soon ceased to exist and was speedily obliterated by the superior power of its adversary.

"There was but one thing wanting to the Confederacy of the South in this respect, and that was the proof of its capacity to cope with its adversary in physical power. We have demonstrated that fact. It is no longer doubt-

Not only did the Yankees call the Southerners "rebels," but there was even a popular Confederate song which featured the term. *Library of Congress.*

ful whether we can maintain our ground against the foe. The doubt has transposed itself to the other side. The question will soon come to be, whether the North can stand up against the South? Ere long, if they do not grant peace, we shall transfer the seat of war to Northern soil. We shall soon have an army in the field large enough to command the city of Washington; and shall dictate from there the terms on which we shall treat with the North. Foreign nations will consider us as already virtually in that position on learning the tidings from Manassas. Recognition is no longer doubtful."

The Confederate Congress seldom released any important news, leaving reporters with nothing to report other than "Congress met at the usual hour, and was opened with a prayer by Rev. Thos. V. Moore. It then went into secret session," or, as another reporter covered it, "Of the proceedings of this body, we know but little." But before its Bull Run session adjourned, the following resolution was adopted: "There is no duty to which our fellow citizens, or their representatives, or agents, are prepared to respond more spontaneously and liberally than to that which summons them to the consolation and relief of their intrepid defenders. It would not become the Congress of the Confederate States to permit the city of Richmond to take to herself the whole charge of providing for the wounded and sick of the army which, under the blessing of Providence, triumphed gloriously at Manassas.... Therefore, be it resolved that the sum of $5,000 be placed at the disposal of the Secretary of the Treasury, to be expended in securing the comfort of the officers and men of the army who were in the battle of Manassas, and may be removed to the city of Richmond."

Wounded, sick, and dying soldiers, Confederate and Union, arrived by every means of transportation. The citizens committee appointed to meet them was constantly in attendance. Crowds, congregating at depots, were implored by every consideration of humanity and fellow feeling for suffering men to fall back and keep out of the way of those who were hastening to remove the helpless soldiers from the cars, otherwise obstructions were thrown in their way which made the work of one hour occupy three and prolonged the weariness and pain of the mangled, wartorn heroes. Since there were corpses, too, on every train, the ill-timed levity of boys and thoughtless men was deplored by soberminded persons, and those in charge requested that all who had no business at such places stay away.

Hospitals and private homes soon were filled; prisons overflowed. The dead were stuffed into boxes for shipment, some being left on the platforms of depots so long that complaints of the stench had to be made to authorities before they were sent on their way. People owning horses and vehicles which were not being used were asked to report the fact to the citizens committee or those in charge of the St. Charles Hospital, so that they could be used in moving the soldiers to places assigned to them. Citizens were also urged to send food already prepared, and

other comforts and delicacies, to the city hospitals or to Manassas, where many of the wounded would have to remain for some time. Supplies for Manassas were to be sent to the store of Spotts & Harvey, on Fourteenth Street, who would forward them. Nearby farmers were asked to furnish the hospitals with all the green vegetables they could spare—"cartloads of peas, potatoes, tomatoes, et cetera." Residents with whom soldiers had been quartered were requested to call on their own physicians, since all had offered gratuitous services for such cases. Any expense which the families could not furnish was to be paid by the committee at the Twenty-fourth Street Hospital. Medical students were asked to aid in duties for which they were qualified such as dressing wounds, putting up prescriptions, and otherwise carrying into effect the treatment directed by the surgeons. They were told it was the best school they could attend, and they would be rendering important services to their country.

The buildings of Chimborazo Hospital covered acres of ground, and more units were added as the war went on and on. *National Archives.*

Efforts were made to help in other ways: "Yesterday the Mayor revived the useful institution of the Chain Gang. His Honor placed several criminals in charge of Officer C. J. Wicker, and ordered him to put them to work at the Post House Hospital where there is much to do in making the place comfortable for the sick soldiers."

One reporter suggested that it would be rendering a service to the public, and especially to the invalid soldiers, to call attention to the fact that in some of the hospitals the cots were of a very inferior quality, having been made so badly that they would not support a man of large size at all, but gave way when he was placed upon one and let him fall to the floor. Who manufactured such beds and sold them to the government was not known, he added, but it was about time to find out and put a stop to such war profiteering.

There was also much criticism of overcrowding in the hospitals and the attention

Buildings within the city were converted into hospitals to meet the urgent need for bed space. *National Archives.*

given captured Yankees who were wounded. The press condemned the practice and said: "As if our own disabled warriors were not sufficient to employ the careful attention of our

Graves of Confederate soldiers, many of whom died from disease, in the old Hollywood Cemetery, Richmond. *Library of Congress.*

physicians and our nurses, a large number of the neglected wounded of the enemy at Manassas has been precipitated upon us to divide the means and comforts, at this sickly season, for the wants and necessities of the sick. There are some five hundred wounded Federalists from the field of Manassas in the hospitals of this city. The ruthless enemy, who thinks the Southern Confederacy of sufficient magnitude to call for immense armies and appropriations to subjugate it, with a mean and contemptible spirit refuses to recognize it as a belligerent power, and will not deign to communicate with our commanders in the usual forms of military etiquette. Standing upon this point, it will neither bury its dead nor take care of its wounded, but leaves both these offices of humanity and Christianity to us rebels, who have our own sick and wounded to take care of and our own dead to bury. This inhumanity of the brutal Northern Government, which merits the bitterest execrations of the civilized world, has given to the field of Manassas horrors hardly excelled in the history of the after-scenes of the great battles of past days.

"We repeat, our hospitals are crowded. Yesterday, two hundred and thirty-two sick and wounded were added by the morning trains. We want, therefore, more room, more nurses, more everything for these soldiers. More private houses, it is hoped, will yet be offered for the accommodation of the increasing numbers. We beg our citizens to continue, and if possible extend, these good offices which, to their lasting praise be it spoken, they have so cheerfully and liberally performed toward our heroes. These gallant men have left their homes and periled their lives, both by the hazards of the field and the greater dangers of disease, in the defense of their country. Not a few of them had stood on the field before the brutalized and drunken army of the North on its march 'to Richmond,' and drove it back, routed and terrified, to the den of the beast of the Northwest, who hounded them on to desolate our land."

Under such crowded conditions, it was inevitable that advertisements such as the following should appear in the newspapers of the Capital:

THE GREAT VIRGINIA REMEDY
AND NO HUMBUG!

PETERS' INFALLIBLE REMEDY FOR
GONORRHEA AND ALL
SECRET DISEASES

People who rushed to the windows when Yankee prisoners were brought into Richmond were openly denounced, but this curiosity probably was aroused by some of the uniforms they wore, such as those of the Zouaves and other foreign-looking outfits like the Hessians.

"Do they think the Yankees have undergone some wonderful transformation of late?" asked one reporter. "Do the ladies and children, who are so eager to get a peep at them, expect to see them armed with wings, or rather with horns and hoofs? They are common enough among us, heaven knows, and there will be plenty more who will require

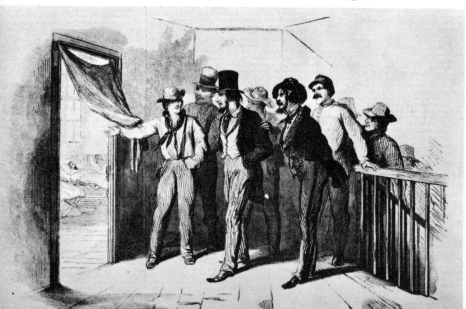

Richmond citizens view a hospital for Yankee prisoners in the Confederate Capital. *Frank Leslie's Illustrated Newspaper.*

"Sketch taken in a southern hotel by several special artists" is the caption on this drawing. *Frank Leslie's Illustrated Newspaper.*

treatment, especially a vast amount of physic and careful attention.

"Complaints are frequently made that some of these Yankee prisoners are treated with too great a degree of leniency. If this be so, the policy is a wrong one. Those now incarcerated here have about as much idea of gratitude, and the way of showing it, as a hog has of polite literature. Are these Yankees to sit here being waited upon and drinking whiskey like old Epicurus? It has been suggested that they be set to work in the trades they know. There must be some first-rate tailors and shoemakers among them who are very anxious for employment. The mortality among them in Richmond is considerable. We regret this for two reasons. First, it gives them no time to repent of their folly and wickedness, and, second, no matter how we treat them, they will invade a territory of fire and brimstone which will make them want to come back here. Colonel Michael Corcoran, late Commander of the famous New York Sixty-ninth Regiment, is now a resident [prisoner] of the city. It is hoped he will have time to reflect on the disadvantages that attend his sojourn here, rendered necessary by the policy of Father Abraham, whom he serves."

But the Yankees didn't want to stay in Richmond, much less come back, and were always trying to escape from hospitals or break out of jail. Some were successful. This gave authorities, both civil and military, additional work to do. Not an hour passed during the day or the night but what some of these "earthworms" were digging their way out to the darkness or banging the guards over the head and making a break for the sunlight. "Six Yankees escaped from the General Hospital on Tuesday night," said one of many similar reports. "They were, of course, convalescent, and took this means of manifesting their gratitude for the kind attention which resulted in putting them on their feet."

There were other disturbances in the city. The little boys who, by their interest in and display of war mimicry, were spoken of as "out-and-out military men" now began to convert their dreams into reality. The attention of city authorities was called to gangs of boys who gathered every evening on a hill overlooking Trinity Church and threw rocks at one another without any consideration of what or whom they hit. The church had been bombarded many times since it had become the "fortress," but fortunately no serious damage had been done. The spot was a few feet outside the city limits and, for that reason, the boys contended the police had no right to

The prison in Richmond where the Yankee Colonel Corcoran was confined. *Frank Leslie's Illustrated Newspaper.*

interfere with them. Other rock battles frequently took place between boys on a hill and those living in the valley. On one occasion several were wounded on each side—all quite seriously. The scene of that battle was near Victor's Mill. "This kind of playful imitation of the more serious engagements of the army of the Potomac," said the press, "seems to be entirely in the hands of our juvenile population. A number of them were brought before the Mayor and ordered to 'keep the peace,' but no one paid any attention to him and the rock battles continue whenever and wherever these boys meet."

Shortly after the second battle of Manassas, the President and his family moved to the Executive Mansion, which had been redecorated and furnished for their comfort. They had three children, Margaret Howell, about seven years old, Jefferson Jr., almost half her age, and Joseph Evan, the youngest then living. Another child, Samuel Emory, had died before the family came to Richmond; in September, 1861, William Howell was born in

the Executive Mansion. Another daughter, Varina Anne, named for her mother, was born there toward the end of the war.

The house stood on the top of a very high hill, sharply defined against the plain at its foot through which ran the Danville railway, leading to the heart of Virginia. The garden, planted in cherry, apple, and pear trees, sloped in steep terraces down the hill to the plain below. The rooms of the house were comparatively few, but very large, some of them more than forty feet square. The ceilings were high, the windows wide, and the stair wells turned in easy curves to the expansive hallways above.

"The Carrara marble mantels were the delight of our children," wrote Mrs. Davis later in life. "One was a special favorite with them, on which the whole pilaster was covered by two lovely figures of Hebe and Diana, one on either side in bold relief, which, with commendable taste, were not caryatids. Our little boys, Jefferson and Joe, climbed up to the lips of these 'pretty ladies' and showered kisses on them. We felt the pleasant sense of being in

Captured Yankees while away the time in a Richmond prison. *Harper's Weekly*.

the house of a cultivated, liberal, fine gentleman, and that he had dwelt here in peaceful interchange of kind office with his neighbors. Mrs. James H. Grant lived in another fine old house next door to us, and with her we formed a lasting friendship, which was testified on her part by every neighborly attention that kind consideration could suggest. If Mr. Davis came riding up the street with General Lee and their staff officers clattering after them, Mrs. Grant heard them and sent some dainty which her housewifely care had prepared, or fruit from her farm on the outskirts of Richmond. If our children were ill, she came full of hope and kind offices to cheer us by her good sense and womanly tenderness. The very sight of her handsome face brought comfort to our hearts. She fed the hungry, visited the sick, clothed the naked, showed mercy to the wicked, and her goodness, like the city set upon the hill, 'could not be hid.'

Jefferson Davis and Mrs. Davis as they appeared before the War. *Confederate Museum.*

South view of the Executive Mansion, Richmond, Virginia. *Confederate Museum.*

Jefferson Davis and Mrs. Davis shortly after the War. *Confederate Museum.*

The Davis children: Jefferson (left) and William with their sisters, Margaret and little Varina Anne, known as "Winnie." *Confederate Museum.*

View from the Executive Mansion at the time it was occupied by the Davis family, looking down upon Shockoe Creek and Butchertown. *Virginia Historical Society.*

"On the plain below the house lived the working class whose sons, known as the Butcher Town Cats, were sworn to eternal enmity against the boys, in the more elegant homes above, who called themselves the Hill Cats. These high contending parties had an hereditary hate which had impelled them for generations to fight, whenever close enough, with either stones or fists. They were the children of the poor against the gentlemen's sons. When the peculiar call whistle adopted by the Hill Cats was heard, they instantly gathered, and, well armed with stones and brick-bats, charged down-hill, let fly their missiles, and beat a double-quick retreat uphill, with the irate Butcher Town Cats at their heels bombarding them in the same fashion."

The President once rescued a little free Negro orphan boy who was being badly treated by some of his own race. He had gone to the Mayor's office and had "free papers" registered so that he would be unmolested by the slaves and other Negro servants at the Executive Mansion. The boy, who called himself Jim Limber every day but became

"Jeemes Henry Brooks" in his Sunday clothes, was a staunch friend of the Hill Cats. "One day he came home with his face covered with blood from a wound received from the Butcher Town Cats," Mrs. Davis continued, "and the President, determined to see if a personal appeal would not quell the warfare, went down the hill and made a little speech to the Butcher Town Cats, calling upon them as the 'future rulers of the country' to keep the peace. The Cats listened respectfully to the end, when their leader stepped to the front and said, 'President, we like you, and we didn't want to hurt any of your boys, but we ain't never goin' to be friends with them Hill Cats.'"

The excitement which now prevailed in the formerly quiet and peaceful city of Richmond confused the residents. Its streets were alive with a multitude of people they had never seen before. Ladies still ventured out in the morning to do their shopping; gentlemen were seen all day, "among them armed thousands, but whither we shall not say," commented a cautious press. Strangers of all sorts seemed to be more firmly rooted than the government. Gamblers, streetwalkers, quack doctors, army deserters, war profiteers, extortionists, counterfeiters, and all the criminal fraternity mingled in public places and crowded law-abiding citizens against the walls. No one knew who was who, and everyone (most of all the police, the Vigilante Committee, and other city authorities) was suspicious of everyone.

The City Council had adopted an ordinance which decreed that persons who knew or suspected others of entertaining, or expressing, subversive sentiments against the Confederate Government were required to inform the Mayor of it. It then would be the Mayor's duty to have such persons arrested, by warrant or otherwise, have them tried, and if found guilty—or there was good reason to believe that they entertained such opinions—to deal with them as vagrants, or persons of evil fame.

Innocent and guilty alike were often confined in the dirty and uncomfortable cells of some guardhouse or hustled off to jail. One of the most discussed of the scores brought in from day to day was Dr. George R. C. Todd. He was living at the St. Charles Hotel when he was arrested and locked up in jail for being a suspicious character and using "incendiary" language. "Todd hails from Lexington, Kentucky," revealed a reporter. "He was heard by sundry witnesses reviling prominent leaders of the Confederate States forces as 'damn traitors,' and indulging in other opprobrious epithets toward the South and its defenders, when he was immediately seized. Prisoner (who has an impediment in his speech) is a brother of Lieutenant David H. Todd, an officer in the service of the Confederate States —a gallant and meritorious gentleman. He is also a brother of Mrs. Lincoln, wife of Abraham Lincoln, President of the Northern States. He had on his person one or more letters franked to him at Lexington, Kentucky, by A. Lincoln, M. C., written, no doubt, when that notorious personage was a Member of the Lower House of Congress; also, a letter of introduction to Governor John Letcher and a letter introducing the bearer to Major Thos.

Hardeman, Second Battalion Georgia Volunteers, near Norfolk. He gave the officer a list of names of persons to summon to prove his character and standing.

"After his arrest, we heard a gentleman declare that Todd had often said to him that he regarded Lincoln as one of the greatest scoundrels unhung, an opinion which (whether really indulged by the Doctor or not) is largely shared in by the people of this section of the country. He was brought before Senior Alderman Sanxay yesterday, and it is but just to him to say that his record as a Southern citizen was proved by the most respectable testimony to be clear and good. The private citizens who arrested Dr. Todd on their motion and without authority of law, yesterday perfectly exonerated him from the charge. He was honorably acquitted, the parties to the transaction expressing their regrets that it had occurred.

"The fact that Dr. Todd is a candidate of a party hostile to our cause, is no reason for suspicion against him. He came four thousand miles to join in our struggle for independence, and proceeds this morning as a volunteer surgeon to aid the wounded at Manassas. If such actions do not prove his faith stronger than words, we do not know what would. We feel unusual regret whenever the precipitate action of any of our citizens have necessitated statements which are afterwards proved to have had their origin in momentary excitement."

The police, the Mayor, government detectives, and all others enforcing the laws were beginning to realize the meaning of overwork. The Honorable Christopher G. Memminger, Secretary of the Treasury, had announced that Confederate bonds had just been issued in sums of five, ten, twenty, and fifty dollars. The bonds were to be received as bank notes by all Southern banks. They were expected to form a very convenient currency, and he hoped the people would readily aid in their circulation. No one was familiar with this currency, and could not easily identify it; consequently the counterfeiters had a field day and flooded the country with bogus money. It was like an epidemic—everybody had it and

The new Confederate currency (above) was unfamiliar in the South, and it was quickly flooded with counterfeit money. *Courtesy of Charles Kohen, Washington, D. C.*

nobody wanted it. A standing joke in Richmond was that to make real money, one had to work in the Treasury Department.

Both innocent and guilty, found with the counterfeit notes, were thrown into jails until they could get a verdict. Thousands stayed there for various lengths of time. Some were never caught. One of the first counterfeit notes to be picked up in the city was passed along to the proprietor of a saloon by "a man dressed as a soldier." He had purchased seventy-five cents' worth of whiskey, paid for it with a twenty-dollar note, and received the correct change. "A pretty good speculation, if you can get away with it," said the barroom owner when he discovered he had been swindled.

To keep up with the times, the big gamblers moved their elaborate equipment into sumptuous quarters. "We spent four days in the Hustings Court of Richmond when one of them was before the Grand Jury for permitting a gambling game commonly called Faro Bank to be exhibited on certain premises," said a reporter. "The Court and jury listened

with patience to the examinations of the witnesses, and the case was elaborately argued by the counsel on both sides. At a late hour on the last evening, the jury retired to consult, but found it impossible to agree upon a verdict, and were discharged. Altogether this legal demonstration against gambling in the city has turned out to be a complete farce. We have no means of ascertaining the precise number of these institutions in Richmond, but will assume there are a hundred. There may be more. Two or three, entered by the police, have had some contraband articles seized, and legal proceedings commenced against them. One unfortunate 'sport' caught in the act, and being minus the means of enlisting the efforts of an able lawyer, was sent to jail for twelve months, and several well-known citizens have forked over small fines which the law imposes upon amateur gamesters; but the leading cases always 'hang fire' in the courts, and the games go on and on with as much vigor as ever. The moral atmosphere still reeks with the taint of 'gambling hells,' and the metropolis of the South makes no advance to that blissful purity so confidently predicted from day to day. We think the gamblers hold all the trumps, and the municipal authorities are up the chimney."

Profiteers and extortioners were busy too. The press complained that gunsmiths, provision merchants, hotel-, restaurant-, and barroom keepers—in fact, all those who had anything to sell—were hiking prices 100 per cent and more on the principle of "keep all you have and get all you can." If such people continue to follow this trend, the press declared, "vox populi will be completely skinned. We are opposed to making money out of the necessities of the people.

"There is scarcely an article of use and necessity which has not been quadrupled in price by grasping speculators, when there is no earthly reason for the unnatural inflation. Patriotic and honorable traders, who have contented themselves with reasonable profits, seem to compose a respectable minority, while speculative combinations give the price to articles of prime necessity, and by the monopoly which they create, throw obstacles in the exercise of that unexampled private liberality which is struggling to furnish supplies to the army. If our forces were able to advance as fast as our prices, the Confederate flag would be now waving in triumph over Niagara Falls."

Flour, wheat, salt, sugar, coffee, butter, eggs, all vegetables and meats were almost beyond the poor man's grasp—but that was exactly what they did, grasp and run. The Mayor had so many cases of petty robberies before him one day that he became disgusted, dismissed court, and went home.

Colder weather brought other problems. Fires were breaking out, usually in small dwellings and shops, caused by defective flues or overheated stoves. But the people became alarmed, fearing they were of incendiary origin. The large number of suspicious characters roaming the streets started rumors that among them were enemy agents trying to accomplish by burning cities, bridges, and communication facilities what the Yankees had been unable to do in open warfare. "Loss by fire is more dreadful than one hundred pitched battles," cried the press. "Unless the authorities are more energetic, what is to save Richmond from such a fate? Some of the deadliest and craftiest enemies of the Government are unquestionably in this 'gay town.'" But the harassed authorities found no one who met that description and fires continued to plague residents and business interests throughout the war.

Frosty mornings were increasing the demand for thick clothing. In anticipation of still greater difficulties in procuring supplies of wood and coal, every prudent citizen was exerting himself to secure enough of such items for the winter. Local officials feared there might be more suffering than usual among the poorer classes, which would call for the attention of the benevolent. It looked as though Richmond were about to become another Valley Forge.

Cold weather and the discomforts of camp life resulted in the desertion of many soldiers from the army. Richmond newspapers were filled with notices such as this: "RETURN AT ONCE!—Having learned that several of my men who were sent from camp to hospital, have left their quarters and gone to Richmond without obtaining leave, I hereby order them to report immediately to me at Camp Defiance, or wherever else I may be stationed.

The caption on this old print reads: "In the midst of life we are in death." *Valentine Museum.*

Part of a typical list of letters to be called for at the city Post Office as published by the Richmond *Dispatch*.

In case of noncompliance, an order will be issued for their arrest wherever found within the Confederate States, when they will be dealt with as confirmed deserters. I forbear naming them at this time as they may be ignorant of their liability to arrest and punishment. G. A. Wallace, Commanding Richmond Light Guard, Virginia Volunteers, Wise Legion." Under another heading, DESERTERS, it was reported that a number of men from the First Virginia Battalion of the Provisional army had not returned to their quarters and that anyone apprehending them would be entitled to a handsome reward. That they had been under the inspiration of a potent spirit did not exempt them as deserters, and, if caught, they would be paid for at so much per head. Out of fifty-eight brought in during the next few days, eight were shot as deserters, and others suffered lighter penalties.

Following these notices were those of persons seeking relatives or friends: "The father-in-law of MR. CHARLES T. STIFF is in this city, and will gladly receive any information of his whereabouts. He is a member of the Twenty-eighth Virginia Regiment, and left Manassas in consequence of sickness. Any information left at the office of THOS. C. C. DREWRY, General Agent and Commission Merchant, next to Columbian Hotel will be thankfully received."

The Post Office was running long columns of names listing uncalled-for mail, and the telegraph company was requesting that messages be collected by the persons referred to in their notices. In the crowded city of Richmond everyone seemed to be lost and looking for other persons who were lost.

The Mayor had returned to his chair, and glanced over the list of persons coming before him. The first was the case of Lizzie Winn, charged with keeping an "ill-governed and disorderly house on May street, where persons assembled for the purpose of lewdness." The Mayor breathed deeply and looked at his crowded courtroom. No matter who was there, all the Mayor could see were little boys throwing rocks, gamblers, extortionists, counterfeiters, all claiming squatters' rights in his city. Now the police were raiding the whorehouses and dragging in the streetwalkers! There was no proof that Lizzie was keeping such a place, and she contended that the girls living there were boarders, poor, out of employment but looking for jobs.

Among the riffraff before the Mayor were others the police had brought in off the streets. A party of six young bloods had taken a notion to have a ride. They climbed on a hack, pommeled the driver with his own whipstock, causing him to jump down from his perch as the carriage drove off in the possession of those who had secured it. Only one of the rowdies was in court. He couldn't remember the incident, was sure there was some mistake; he had just arrived in the city and didn't know five other people in the whole place. His case was dismissed. A hack driver had driven his horses at a furious pace up Main Street while drunk, said the police. Near Nineteenth Street, he turned the horses quickly, fell off the seat, "and achieved the remarkable feat of driving his carriage over himself as he lay sprawling in the mud." The hack driver contended it was a cold day, that he was driving his horses to keep them warm when the accident occurred; he had hurt no one but himself and, therefore, there was no reason to have hauled him into court. The charge against him was dropped. "A jolly old fellow who had been courting Bacchus" was accused of loudly hurrahing in a barroom for Lincoln and the Yankee Republicans. He said he meant no harm by doing so, that he had two sons serving under Johnston and Beauregard, and begged leniency of His Honor for the sake of his two sons, who would be mortified if they heard that their father had been drinking again. He was warned about his behavior and dismissed.

Michael Leary was before the Mayor for threatening to chastise Ann O'Riley. There was some testimony about the woman having broken into a tenement rented by Leary, where she domiciled herself and went to housekeeping in spite of all efforts to eject her. "The whole case was made as clear as mud to the understanding of the reporters there," wrote one who was covering the proceedings.

After several hours of getting nowhere with

Long columns of "Personals" asking information of relatives or friends also appeared in the Richmond *Dispatch*.

such cases, His Honor delivered some sound lectures to the spectators and parties present, declaring it his determined purpose to maintain the majesty of the law and the dignity of his old commonwealth. He said, however, that it was almost impossible to get at the truth in regard to anything and not easy to have the individuals identified as having been present, or having taken part in incidents, and, therefore, court was dismissed for the day. The Mayor looked really ill to newsmen and seemed to be going crazy as a result of the situation.

Reporters were also putting into print what they thought of their jobs. "We are sick of the work of recording the rows of soldiers," one confessed. "Another big fight took place near the corner of Twelfth and Cary streets last night. A file of soldiers and a large body of police were on the spot. The soldiers were hunting up their missing comrades, and, when near our office on their return, some gentlemen on the corner impudently made a remark, which one of the soldiers took in high dudgeon, and a terrible battle of words and fists was the result." Another reported a frightful scene of disorder, confusion and terror, pistols fired, oaths and threats uttered, on Seventeenth Street near the Old Market. The police succeeded in carrying off some ten of the rowdies to jail, and a file of men, under the lieutenants of the Public Guard, was detailed to keep guard over them during the night. "A beautiful spectacle it is to see our civil prisons threatened by rowdy soldiers, when their officers have plenary power to keep them in camp, and we are astonished that the military should allow such desperate characters to roam over the city by day and by night. We are mortified in making such remarks; and so much ashamed of the performances of some of our soldiers that we have been trying to persuade ourselves, and our readers, that the scoundrels in uniform were not soldiers at all, but imposters. Nothing but our duty to the public impels us to indulge in such language. And we think it time for plain words when the military has to be ordered out to suppress disorder in our streets."

There were so many fatalities, including those of the war, that J. D. Gatewood advertised for more workmen "accustomed to making coffins" at his factory on Broad Street. Richmond officials, too, tried to take care of this overflow by improving and enlarging the burial place. According to one resident, "the establishment of a new Hollywood Cemetery and its opening to the public marked the pathway of our advancement as a city, though, like all improvements, it was at first vigorously and determinedly opposed. Now, everybody is in favor of it. It is a treasury filled with grand and holy memories—a little Eden garnished with flowers—the offerings of affection on the altar of memory, roofed by trees planted by nature and art, and glorious in its loveliness. All, therefore, should seek more and more to make it what its founders intended it to be originally—an ornament to our city. It is better adapted for the use to which it has been devoted than any other similar piece of ground we know anywhere. The murmuring waters of the James River sound a perpetual requiem to the memory of the dead entombed above them."

Guns boomed again, and the news of battles in Missouri reached Richmond. Confederate forces had been routed at Wilson's Creek, and General Nathaniel Lyon, leading a charge at the head of his column, had been killed. There was no better news at the end of August when General B. F. Butler captured Fort Hatteras in North Carolina and drove out the Confederate troops. It was Butler who took possession of slaves as property under the law, claiming that they were contraband of war, and thus established that name for them. To people of the South, Butler was "the beast" in public, and a host of unprintable names in private.

People were getting out their winter clothing, sleeping under blankets, and crying to state authorities, "Don't call out the militia; such a wholesale requirement will rob us of help and stop the wheels of industry!" Though exempted from a call into immediate service, members of the militia were required to muster once a week, and were liable to be fined for being absent under the provisions of a proclamation by Governor Letcher.

Contraband of War
First Contraband Article: "Why, Julius, what's goin' to become ob de cullud pop'lation in dis War? Heah's dis chile been mor'n sebenty yeahs one ob de cullud race, an' been called a *niggah*, a *chattels*, an *institution*, an' now he's a *contraban'*. I s'pose de out-cum will be dis nigger will lose his position on de face ob de airth altogether—dat's so!" *Harper's Weekly.*

Theaters were opening, and at one of the early performances at the Metropolitan Hall a song, "God Will Defend the Right," was heard for the first time. It was composed by an unnamed young lady of Richmond who had "just returned from Germany after several years' hard study under the best masters." Since the outbreak of war, many of the popular Southern actors had gone to Europe, Joseph Jefferson and E. A. Sothern among them. The Richmond Theatre promised the great actress, Ida Vernon, and others—with Clementine DeBar, daughter of Junius Brutus Booth, Jr. (brother of Edwin and John Wilkes), featured as a member of the company—for the winter season. Formerly known as the Marshall Theatre, all the great British and American actors had played there, including the elder Booth when he first arrived from England in 1821. Available at the Confederate Reading Room was a great variety of books, magazines, and newspapers, some from the Northern states. One of these was the *New York Herald* containing the false report of President Davis's death.

How the rumor started no one knew, but

the *Herald* stated it was true. "Our latest telegraphic advices from Louisville, Washington, and Fortress Monroe, assure us positively of the death of Jefferson Davis, Provisional President, or Dictator rather, of our rebellious Confederate States," declared the *Herald.* "Considering that his health has been in a very shattered condition for several years, and considering his extraordinary labors, anxieties, and exhausting excitements of the last five months, we were not only prepared to believe the report of his death, but we think it somewhat remarkable that he was not carried off three or four months ago. Assuming that he has at length gone the way of all the earth, the first question suggested is: What will be the effect of his loss to the bad cause of this Southern rebellion?

"We think that the loss of Davis at this time will be more serious to the rebel cause than would have been the defeat of Beauregard at Bull Run. Davis was the man of all the aspiring leaders of the South for the post of Pro-

One of General Butler's "Contraband of War" captured at Fort Hatteras, "sketched by a special artist accompanying Butler's Command." *Frank Leslie's Illustrated Newspaper.*

The Richmond Theatre, where many great stars of the time, both from the North and South, appeared during the War. *Valentine Museum.*

visional Dictator of the rebel States. Educated as a soldier at West Point, his conduct at the battle of Buena Vista rendered him exceedingly popular throughout the South as a military chieftain. His subsequent prominent career as a Southern partisan leader in the United States Senate, and in the Cabinet of poor Pierce, as Secretary of War, and again as the anointed champion of the Mississippi disunionists in the Senate at Washington, had given him a character in the cotton States for statesmanship and administrative talents fully up to the standard of his military reputation.

"Thus combining the practical training and knowledge and popularity of the regular soldier with a very large experience as a fire-eating politician, legislator, and executive civil officer, State and Federal, Davis was the very man required as the Provisional head of this desperate experimental Southern Confederacy. Self-conceited, self-willed, arrogant and despotic, we have in these peculiarities of Davis the very qualities which, of all others, were most needful to enable him to give force

and authority to his position as President of the Confederate States. He was invested with this office because of these very qualities, and because the crude, loose, and irresponsible embryo Government of which he was the chief, and the exigencies of the armed rebellion with which was associated, demanded a dictator. He was named the President, but the few men who thus appointed him, did not expect him to assume the powers of an absolute despot.

"Thus we can account for the wonderful military energy, activity and resources brought into the field by the rebel States. They have been called into requisition by Davis, the absolute despot of the new confederation. We anticipate the question:— Was he not subject to the laws of the Confederate Congress? by answering that the Congress, consisting of only one house, of from twenty to thirty self-appointed disunion managers, was nothing more than the obedient *corps legislatif* of the Southern Dictator. They legislated according to his will, and all his subordinates, military and civil, were taught, before appointed, the necessity of absolute obedience to their chief. Our readers will thus comprehend to some extent the loss to the rebel cause of this man Davis, with his great popularity, his abilities and industrious habits, his unbounded authority and his dictatorial character."

Richmond editors played up the report as an example of Yankee delusion and the unreliability of all news in the Northern press. They referred to the *Herald* as the "most mendacious journal in the world" with a record for lying second to none. With one statement in the *Herald* they agreed: Considering the extraordinary labors, anxieties and exhausting excitement of the last five months, it was remarkable that the President was still alive.

Also very much alive, and bearing the President's name, was the Jeff Davis Artillery, a company of volunteers from Alabama. After being reviewed by the President, the men had paraded through the streets with guns, caissons, and everything else ready for duty on the battlefield. Another tribute to the President was the new stamp bearing his features with the words CONFEDERATE STATES OF AMER-

Courtesy of Charles Kohen, Washington, D. C.

ICA above and FIVE CENTS below. The issue had been delayed in order to procure an engraving "not liable to be counterfeited, which is so easy where there is no engraving on steel to be had." On October 16, 1861, the first one was sold in Richmond.

A new and more suitable hall for the deliberations of Congress was now ready for their sessions. The former Senate Chamber, lobby, and Clerk's office had been transformed into a large and spacious interior by the removal of the walls and galleries. The hall had been furnished with elegantly upholstered furni-

The Battle of Wilson's Creek. *Frank Leslie's Illustrated Newspaper.*

ture and a handsome carpet. The members congratulated themselves upon the prospect of a place where they could enjoy the *odium cum dignitate* undisturbed by the presence of abolition orators and "small beer politicians."

The President, in his message to Congress that November, protested the seizure, by Captain Charles Wilkes of the United States naval vessel *San Jacinto*, of James M. Mason and John Slidell, passengers on the British vessel *Trent*. "The distinguished gentlemen, whom, with your approval, at the last session," said Mr. Davis, "I commissioned to represent the Confederacy at certain foreign courts, have been recently seized by the captain of a United States ship-of-war, on board a British steamer, traveling from the neutral Spanish port of Havana to England. The United States has thus claimed a general jurisdiction over the high seas, and entering a British ship, sailing under its country's flag, violated the rights of embassy, for the most part held sacred even amongst barbarians, by seizing our Ministers whilst under the protection and within the dominions of a neutral nation." Most Confederate leaders expected the affair to draw the United States into a war with Great Britain but, in time, it was amicably settled.

Little news of General Lee was being published except that he was at Sewell Mountain in Western Virginia with a sufficient number of troops to hold his position should he be attacked. Mr. Davis was still the man in the spotlight.

"Notwithstanding that the reign of Sirius is past," wrote a reporter, "we are having dog-days again. The dog catchers are out, spreading their nets to capture the little beasts, of high and low degree, who howl, bark, and bite. It is a rather pitiful sight, however, to see the imprisoned animals looking sorrowfully through the bars of their cage as they move on to the place of execution. The captive Yankees, gazing wistfully from the windows of our tobacco factory [Libby Prison] do not excite so much commiseration in the human breast."

That the Yankees who were out of prison had been up to some mischief was certain in reports that the Federals had captured Port Royal Harbor in South Carolina, established a South Atlantic base on Hilton Head Island, and repulsed a Confederate attack on Fort Pickens at Pensacola, Florida.

Such gloomy news was somewhat offset by the opening of a large laboratory "which had sprung into existence, almost as if by magic," for repairing and refitting muskets. It was located on Eighth Street and owned by the Confederate Government. Two large steam engines furnished the power and many employees, experts in their trade, were working day and night in their special divisions. "This should be encouraging," noted the press, "to those who suppose that the Government is not pushing forward vigorously in every respect, with a determined resistance against the foe." A large number of muskets, thrown away by the Yankees on their flight from Manassas, were undergoing repairs and leaving the hands of the workmen "good as new." Every citizen who possessed an old gun for which he had no special use was asked to serve the cause of the South by sending it in to the Ordnance Department. The press also advised that persons who had collected trophies from the battlefields take heed of the notice published in the Richmond newspapers which read:

"There are thousands of arms, muskets, rifles, pistols, swords, and carbines—the property of the Confederate States, having been captured from the United States, which are in the hands of citizens throughout the Confederacy, and are held by them as trophies. The most urgent need of these arms, every one of them, old and new, good and bad, broken and sound, is upon us. For every one of them a volunteer is kept out of the field or sent to risk his life with a fowling piece or a flintlock. Money will not supply their places; they were bought with blood, and their absence from the field will surely cost us more blood. All having these arms, or even parts of them, are implored to return them at once, and magistrates and police officers everywhere are requested to apply the law to those having neither honesty or patriotism. Let all 'trophies' be shipped immediately by ex-

Messrs. Mason and Slidell, Confederate Commissioners, are seized on board the British mail-steamer *Trent* by Captain Wilkes of the U. S. warship *San Jacinto*. *National Park Service*.

Quarters for Yankee officers in Libby Prison and sketches of two captains interned there. *Valentine Museum*.

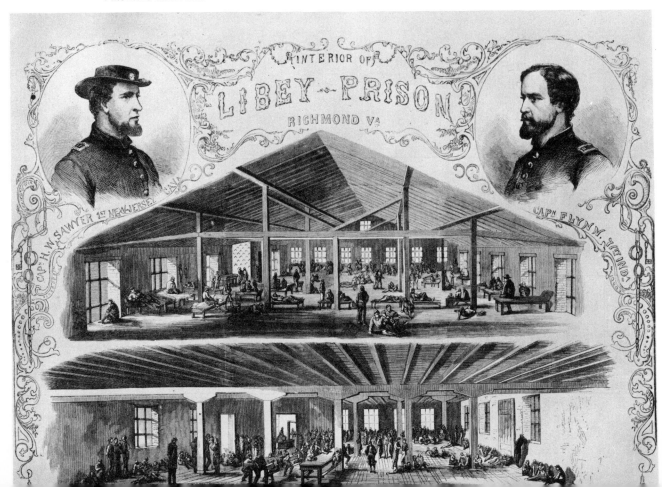

Relics such as these preserved in the Confederate Museum, Richmond, were considered the choicest of "trophies."

press to 'Ordnance Officer, Manassas Junction,' where charges on them will be paid.

E. P. ALEXANDER,
Chief Ord. A. P."

With winter not far distant, more and more of the 1,500 Yankee prisoners then in Richmond were being exchanged by flag-of-truce boats plying between there and Newport News. The majority of the Yankees had lost a leg or an arm, or were so disabled by wounds that they were unfit for further military service. An equal number of Confederate soldiers, likewise disabled, was returning to the city. This operation meant only a slight fluctuation in its population from time to time, without any real relief of its overcrowded conditions. The Confederate soldiers who were discharged and left for their own homes were always replaced by others as the War between the States went on and on through the years.

Despite a bad cold the President reviewed one of the most imposing military spectacles ever seen in Richmond. It was held on a field adjoining the Hollywood Cemetery and was attended by government officials, high-ranking officers of the Confederate forces, and many pretty ladies. The new Battle Flag of the Confederacy waved above the crowd and was carried by the troops on the field. Their movements were finely executed, particularly when ordered to charge. The horses were not

only remarkable for their quality and condition, but their training had been excellent. Mr. Davis expressed himself as highly pleased with the efficiency and unexceptionable appearance of the command, adding that no enemy on earth ever could conquer men so inspired and so loyal to the South.

This overconfidence of the people and their

90

leaders was spurred by a Confederate victory at Ball's Bluff, but Lee was still in his mountain fastness of Western Virginia, where rains and bad roads prevented any real action against Yankee General W. S. Rosecrans. For a time "General Mud" took over on most fronts, and the people of Richmond felt secure from attack so long as he was in charge.

The local news reported that Paul Morphy was exhibiting his skill at the Richmond Chess Club, gas had been installed at the penitentiary, giving the gloomy place an unusually cheerful appearance, and the Clerk's register showed that more marriage licenses were being issued than ever before. The last item drew the attention of a reporter, who commented: "Whether bacon is twelve or twenty-five cents a pound, and boots eight or sixteen dollars a pair; no matter what is the price of calico or fine linen, or the expense of house rent, young people will continue to form al-liances matrimonial, and take upon their inexperienced shoulders, the responsibilities of wedded life. Love rules the court, the camp, and the grove."

The increased cost of production, bemoaned the Richmond press, made it necessary to advance the price for newspapers. Apparently this resulted in many subscribers not paying their bills or being slow in doing so. "Newspaper subscriptions are infallible tests of a man's honesty," said one. "If he is dishonest, he will cheat the printer some way—says he has paid what he has not, declares he has the receipt somewhere, or sent money and it was lost in the mail. Or he will take the paper and not pay for it on the grounds that he did not subscribe for it, or will move off, leaving it coming to the office he has left. Thousands of professed Christians are dishonest, and the printer's book will tell fearful tales in the final judgment."

Confederate prisoners, many of whom were exchanged for Yankee prisoners on flag-of-truce boats. *National Archives.*

The field adjoining Hollywood Cemetery was the scene of all important reviews by high-ranking officers such as this one by General Beauregard. *Illustrated London News.*

Retreat of Federal troops after the fight at Ball's Bluff, upper Potomac, Virginia. *Illustrated London News.*

Another day of fasting and prayer was observed in the Capital. General Lee had returned for a conference with the President, then left for Beaufort, South Carolina, charged with the command of the coast defenses south of Virginia. Several Confederate naval officers had accompanied him.

A Grand Dramatic Ethiopian Entertainment of Burlesques, Farces, Solos, Choruses, Singing and Dancing was playing to large audiences at the Richmond Varieties—and the Mayor's Court was doing likewise. The Confederate Collector of the War Tax was asking editors to remind citizens, by printing notices in their newspapers, that payment was due, and it was "their duty, in times like the present, to fork over the 'sinews of war' without grumbling."

On Thanksgiving day the happiness of former years was not so evident in the City of the Seven Hills. Many homes had empty chairs at the table; their loved ones were far away at camps. One of these was General Howell Cobb, who had presided over the Provisional Congress but now was with his troops on the Peninsula. His former duties were in the hands of Vice-President Alexander H. Stephens, who was too frail and sickly to be in the military service.

But Richmond people did have one thing for which to be thankful. General W. T. Sherman and his Yankee troops were far away too—running over South Carolina with fire and sword. "We are astonished," said an editorial, "that he could accept the command of an expedition destined to lay waste the homes where he had been a welcome guest, and to make widows and orphans of the women and children who, through eight years of his residence among them, made him forget that he was a stranger." Reports that orders had been issued prohibiting the destruction of cotton in danger of falling into the hands of the enemy were denied by the commanding officers of Confederate forces at points along the coast, who had instructions to burn any and all property which could not be conveniently taken away and was likely to be seized by the invaders.

Disturbances in Richmond were of less concern, yet more immediate. Ida Vernon, the favorite of all residents in the Capital, had opened in *Camille* at the Richmond Theatre. During the evening a "discordant gibble" in the gallery disturbed others who were interested in the performance. Several persons cried out "Keep quiet!" and the parties rushed at one another while some in the audience crawled over the seats to watch the fight. It all began and ended so suddenly that no one was sure who had really started the row. "The reckless individuals who patronize the amusement places in our city," noted one editorial, "are disgusting in the extreme, and make one wish that Richmond was still the provincial village it was years ago. Since its sudden transformation to a mighty metropolis, it has attracted a sort of surplus population not very beneficial to its social character or standing. If people want to fight, why don't they go to an open field where they will have plenty of room and not disturb others?"

Several persons followed the editor's advice and settled their differences with an "affair of honor." One took place at the Broad Rock Race Course on the south side of the James River. Messrs. Washington Worsham and John McCullough, "of the sporting fraternity," had a misunderstanding in regard to a business matter. Worsham had challenged McCullough to a duel and was accepted. The two men, with a number of friends and several surgeons, met at the appointed place early one morning. The duel was fought with pistols, at a distance of ten paces. The shots were simultaneous, and both men fell, badly wounded. McCullough, who was from New Orleans, was taken to his hotel, and eventually recovered. Worsham was removed to his residence on Sixth Street, where he died.

Another duel was fought during November between a Doctor Forward and a Lieutenant Jones of the Fifth Louisiana Regiment. They also met just outside the city limits. The weapons were Mississippi rifles, and the distance forty paces. Both men fired at the same time, and both fell. Jones was killed instantly, and Forward died a few minutes later. Their bodies were brought back to Richmond and forwarded to their homes. No action was taken

against any survivors of such duels reported at various periods during the war. The good old days of Southern chivalry had returned to thrill the descendants of an era believed to have passed away.

While people were talking of the mild weather Richmond had enjoyed for several days, saying that if it continued there would be no brandy left for "smashes" the next summer, it began to snow. "With the last month of the year half gone, we are jogging along pretty rapidly toward Christmas," noted one reporter, "and a lack of really cold weather has brought serious discussions of the ice question by residents of this city. Whether or not the war continues, we want to be independent of the North in this respect, and, as we shall probably have a hard freeze ere long, we hope every man who has the means of doing so, will pack away a good supply of ice. It will be needed in the hospitals."

The approaching holidays were causing a stampede at railroad stations by homeward-bound civilians, soldiers on furlough, and others wishing to buy tickets. All complained that the time between the arrival of the ticket agent and the departure of the trains was so short that it was impossible for many of them to be accommodated. Amid this brief and hurried period the furlough papers and transportation tickets of the military had to be looked

over, shinplasters (Confederate currency notes of small value) to be tested, discussed, changed, or rejected, and passports examined. With elbowing, curses, treading on corns, doing business in a squeeze through a hole about twelve inches square, while trembling for fear that a train would start off and leave one packed among a dozen stalwart forms—the scene was too awful to be described, and too annoying to be endured, protested the travelers. "Is there no remedy?" they asked. If not, they had suggestions for the railroad officials.

Many passengers were at the ticket office long before it was opened. If the agent were there and it opened earlier, so much of the trouble they had to endure would not be crowded into the last minutes, spent in fear of being stranded at the station. Lives were often imperiled by travelers' attempts to get on the trains as they were moving away. All their complaints fell upon deaf ears; each holiday the same scene was enacted, until the people themselves finally despaired of changing it.

Everyone in Richmond was preparing for Christmas. In spite of high prices, women were at the markets buying turkeys, beef roast, cranberries, plum puddings, and confections, and "fixins" of all sorts. "The annual visit of Santa Claus," said the press, "cannot be prevented by the blockade. If some think we should not be merry because many of our dear friends are away at camp or in the field, they are mistaken. Surely, we may have our pleasures at home as heretofore. We can pledge the cup of kindness to the boys away from home, who will be the happier for the good wishes and tender thoughts of them around the family hearthstones. There is no more harm now than in former days in extending the good old greeting to all:

"We wish you a Merry Christmas,
And a Happy New Year;
A pocket full of money,
And a cellar full of beer."

At Franklin Hall, near the Exchange Hotel, and at the William Tell House, on Broad Street, various entertainments were given for collecting funds to buy food and gifts for men in the nearby camps, and many residents in the city invited at least one soldier, away from his own fireside, to dine with them on Christmas day. During the afternoon and evening, the young people went to the theater and other places of amusement but their elders remained at home, "not having any social benefits to gain from such excursions." There were many parents who had only letters from their sons to comfort them that day. One of these read:

Dear Folks:

A Happy Christmas to you all from a quiet line of the army. Yankee General McClellan has no idea of taking Christmas cheer down on this little old stream called Bull Run. We are sorry for that, while, with creamy bowl of eggnog, we soldiers drink permanency to the young Confederacy, and the good health to our glorious President, Jefferson Davis.

Imitating the example of the "Zouaves of the Crimea and Algeria," our boys in camp contrive to invent ways and means to relieve the monotony of our present existence by the agreeable introduction of theatricals. We have just received from them the program of a dramatic performance for our amusement on Christmas Eve. The leading play for the occasion is the "Maniac Avenger," in which several distinguished actors (in the language of the show-bills generally) "make their first appearance in this place." Then there

is to be a banjo player and some singers who will give us other novelties.

The only new thing of note, is a custom recently adopted in the army. When a worthless soldier is "drummed out," it is done to the tune of "Yankee Doodle" instead of the "Rogue's March," as was the custom. This new custom arose from the fact that more rogues march any day, nowadays, to the tune of "Yankee Doodle," than have marched in all time, to the "Rogue's March." The custom arose from a suggestion of Colonel Harry Haze, of the Seventh Louisiana Regiment, and does that gentleman credit as an observer of events.

God bless and keep all of you is the prayer of your son,

CLAIBORNE

Yankees in one military prison, as a reporter passed by on Christmas day, "were in a high state of enjoyment, singing, laughing and shouting, as if their present position was an improvement upon anything they had been accustomed to at home. The prisoners of rank, confined on the lower floor of one of the buildings, looked rather more sedate." Whiskey and the holiday spirit affected at least two men, one arrested for shooting off firecrackers in the Second Market, the other for shooting off a pistol in the street.

A philosophical mood or a hangover (probably a combination of both) prompted a reporter to write: "Some of the more prominent characteristics of the Christmas holidays have been visible all about for a day or two past. The eggnog must have had an undue proportion of bad whiskey, judging from the very common complaint of misery in the head or somewhere else. Some of our acquaintances, who boast that they were never before 'thrown,' have been forced to acknowledge

A "shinplaster," also known as "fractional currency." *Courtesy of Charles Kohen, Washington, D. C.*

the corn this Christmas, and now feel conscious of having done some very foolish things, which they can't exactly describe. These holiday indulgences, moreover, are dangerous and expensive. They make people sick, and the man who gets sick nowadays must pay the doctor a dollar and a half for feeling his pulse. In other respects, the present season varies from the holiday peculiarities of former years. There are fewer idle negroes about the streets, and people who were wont to keep it up for a week are now reflecting upon the ways and means to keep body and soul together."

On New Year's Eve, the people of Richmond gathered in their homes to say good-bye to 1861. Many spoke of it as the most eventful year of the present century; all agreed that the times demanded a more serious and sober contemplation of the future than had been given to the past. Those who had imbibed too freely at Christmas made the usual resolutions—then forgot them. Public places were noisy and rowdy, the "strangers frolic," as it was called, being prolonged into the New Year. Police carried off the most boisterous and inebriated of the merry-andrews so they could meet more soberly in the Mayor's Court at the proper time. The most unhappy person in Richmond was a reporter. Under the heading LOCAL OBSERVATIONS, he wrote:

"Of all the grief that harasses the distressed, sure the most bitter is a quiet day, when the patient 'Local' wanders east and west, yet never finds an item in his way; neither incident, accident, fire or fight, murder or suicide, from morning till night. Yesterday was one of the days on which, as a celebrated classic writer has observed, incidents were as scarce as hen's teeth. Speaking of hens reminds us of a Shanghai fowl which we saw last week; it had four legs (as sure as eggs is eggs) and we should like to have some naturalist tell us what particular species the creature belongs to. So well furnished was it with the means of locomotion, that it must have been a Yankee, at all events. With regard to Yankees, we may state that there were twelve fresh arrivals at the prisons yesterday, but there is no very strong anxiety for any

more of that sort of game. The luxury is too expensive in these times. If anybody wants to find out anything about the price of luxuries, of the domestic kind, let him go through our city markets early in the morning. If he be a bachelor, it may settle his opinion very suddenly upon the subject of matrimony; for however much of romance and bliss there may be in wedded life, one cannot divest his mind of the practical truth that wives and children must eat. Speaking of children reminds us that the holidays are almost over, and the now vacant schoolhouses will very soon resound with the prattle of tiny voices, almost baffling the patient pedagogue's efforts to teach the young how to shoot. We have some sharply disciplined schools, with accomplished teachers and myriads of pupils, devoted to that particular branch of experimental science; and the experience of the *past year* has shown that the practice has not been entirely thrown away.

"Yet, while the weather offers every advantage for a fight, the Yankees remain in their strongholds, and give our men no chance to present them with Southern farms—six feet by two. A remark upon the weather brings up the ice question. The ponds have frozen over for two or three nights past, but the midday sun dissolved the ice, and dissipates all prospect of brandy smashes next summer; while the boys look with despair upon their rusty and long-unused skates. Still, it is some advantage to have open navigation even though there is not much doing in that line. Cargoes of wood constantly arrive, but are generally used for army purposes. Oyster boats, too, come in occasionally, and the market is pretty well supplied. Prices seem to be regulated by the demand, which has been immense during the whole season, so dealers find no difficulty in fixing their own 'figures.' We believe everybody likes *oysters,* and will have them, no matter what the cost. It is dangerous for an individual to drink too much while on his way to inspect the oyster fleet (of two boats) as one did yesterday. He was badly beaten by somebody, and the officers picked him up and carried him to the cage. There was no other arrest during the day that we could hear of.

It was a very quiet day—a great many sturdy soldiers (not always steady, though) about the streets—a great many ladies promenading —and a great many cheerful faces, notwithstanding the Northern barbarians assume that Richmond presents a picture of despair."

The year 1861 set the pattern Richmond was to follow during the War between the States. Its crowded streets, hotels, hospitals, prisons; its transportation facilities always filled to capacity with soldiers and civilians traveling about at a furious pace; its factories turning out war materials; its thousands of government employees scattered everywhere; its Negro problems, slave and free; its unwelcome criminal fraternity—speculators, counterfeiters, and all the other riffraff; had been catalogued by its press. And those who hoped that the once quiet, peaceful, and orderly Capital of the State of Virginia, and of the new Confederacy, would grow into a thriving center of industrial life had their wish. The City of the Seven Hills had become the Metropolis of the South.

Game and barrels of oysters on sale in Richmond.
Richmond Times-Dispatch.

"Fellow Citizens--"

New Year's Day 1862 was bright and beautiful, although the breeze stirred up the dust considerably. Two notable events attracted Richmond residents: the President's reception and the one given by Governor Letcher. The first was held from twelve until three o'clock in the afternoon and those attending, including many pretty ladies, looked very gay and cheerful. The President stood at the door of a large reception room where thousands of persons gave him a friendly grasp of the hand. Mrs. Davis was not present, but her place was taken by her sister, Miss Margaret Graham Howell. The ceremonies of introduction were conducted by the President's aides, Colonel Joseph R. Davis, his nephew, and Colonel G. W. Custis Lee, eldest son of General Lee. Eggnog and other "compounds peculiar to the winter festivities" were by no means forgotten. The Armory Band was present, and everything passed off delightfully. An hour later, Governor Letcher received his guests at the Mansion in Capitol Square.

That evening, the Richmond Theatre, pride of the city, burned to the ground. In a short time after the alarm was given, the entire building was in flames, and when the first engine arrived it was found impossible to do much else than try to save the adjoining property. But even these efforts failed to protect two smaller buildings which went up in smoke and several others which were partially damaged. The theater contained many valuable furnishings, all the stage equipment for the production of Shakespeare and other classical plays, orchestral instruments, music, and personal property of the actors and people employed there. Nothing but the walls were left early the next morning and one of those fell, taking some telegraph wires with it. People were advised to walk on the other side of the street if they didn't want their brains dented by brickbats. No lives were lost in the fire, but while the crowd gazed at the smoldering ruins, a runaway horse, with a wagon attached, dashed by at a furious pace and several people were injured in a stampede for places of safety.

Fires had not been made in the theater stoves that night, and it was thought that the flames had been started by an incendiary. While the theater was burning, a member of the orchestra went into the alleyway, hoping he could save some of his possessions, and found a window open. The clue led to someone else who had seen a Negro crawl out of the window, before the fire started, but had done nothing about detaining him. Muskets had been used in the play that evening, but the manager had remained for more than an hour after the performance, so it was said the fire could not have started from that source. All investigations proved fruitless, and the cause of the fire was never discovered.

Manning the batteries in and around Richmond had prompted the Governor to organize a regiment of citizens who had objected to serving elsewhere because of family and busi-

Map of Richmond, Petersburg, and vicinity showing the James River, railroads, and battlegrounds. *National Archives.*

first having been at Manassas (Bull Run). Meanwhile, the Richmond press was to report Confederate defeats at Mill Springs, Kentucky, Fort Henry, Fort Donelson, and Nashville, Tennessee, and much other bad news for Mr. Davis.

The death of John Tyler, former President of the United States and late member of the Confederate Congress from Virginia, was mourned by all people in the South. To them he had been a great and good man, whom they had loved, venerated, and trusted more than any other statesman. The moment his death was announced, government offices in Richmond were closed, flags were lowered to half-mast and some buildings draped with mourning. The following day, his remains were taken to the Hall of Congress to lie in state surrounded by an honor guard from his native Virginia.

On the day of the funeral (January 20), the President and members of Congress gathered to pay their final respects to the man whose voice would no more be heard in the councils of his country. With the Hall filled to overflowing, Congress was called to order, and a fervent prayer was offered by the Rev. Dr. Moses Drury Hoge, who alluded in fitting terms to the character of the man whose death was recognized as a calamity for the Confederacy. Several members of Congress spoke of the great services he had rendered the country, and the melancholy bereavement all had felt when his death occurred. A resolution was passed; in honor of the illustrious statesman, members of Congress would wear a badge of mourning for thirty days, and the family of the deceased be notified of its proceedings.

Despite unfavorable weather, Capitol Square was crowded as the casket was removed from the Hall to the hearse, to be conveyed to nearby St. Paul's Episcopal Church. Preceded by the Police Guard, whose band played a solemn dirge, the hearse was followed by carriages in which rode President Davis, Governor Letcher, the members of Congress, the Virginia Senate, the House of Delegates, and prominent citizens. There Bishop John Johns spoke of the personal

ness affairs in the city. Since the militia had not been called out, they were to enlist as volunteers for twelve months, with the requirement that they be trained and ready at all times to defend the Capital. The ranks were quickly filled, and soon they began drilling and parading through the streets.

In the years to follow, Virginia was to become the real battleground of the War between the States. Of the six great battles to be fought by Confederate troops, three more were to be on her soil, making four in all, the worth and virtues of the lamented dead and conducted the impressive burial service of the Episcopal church. The remains were then borne to Hollywood Cemetery and laid to rest near the tomb of James Monroe.

Since his last message, the President told Congress, events had demonstrated that the government had attempted more than it had the power successfully to achieve. The fall of Fort Donelson and other defeats, and the policy of short-term enlistments—which he had opposed—had contributed to these reverses. When the war first broke out, many of the Southern people could not be persuaded that it would be a long war. With so vast a territory to defend and protect, but destitute of the means for doing so, the South was totally dependent upon the valor and devotion of its people. They must realize, he repeated, that the road ahead of them would not be an easy road to travel.

But some of the people continued to think more of personal gain than of their homeland. "The merchants of Richmond undoubtedly gathered in a harvest since the commencement of the war," stated the press, "and it is the wonder of many persons how they manage to keep the stock of dry goods replenished. Passing along the business streets, we see bales and boxes in profusion, and there never has been a time when the feminine portion of the community dressed in more elaborate style than at present. If there was in the Southern Confederacy, when the ports were closed, a supply sufficient to last forever, the purchases of 1860 must have been enormous. It is hinted that goods are smuggled in from the North, and Southern gold goes over the line to pay for them, even now; but we hesi-

tate about believing such imputation. Nevertheless, there is something mysterious about the matter, which possibly may be brought to light some of these days."

Another reporter argued that if the blockade against Southern ports could be broken, it would cause a terrible havoc among the extortioners in all branches of business, and the vast variety of articles stored away would crawl out from hiding places to be offered to the public at moderate prices. Even the Salt Works might then fill orders waiting so long to be supplied, and bring down the cost from ten dollars to the normal price of seventy-five cents a bushel. Everyone in Richmond cried out that the blockade could not be broken too soon for the good of the community, except the monopolists and the extortioners.

With cold winds blowing, and dark clouds hanging over the city, residents woke up one morning to read that owing to the scarcity of gas and the want of material to set retorts, gas would be turned off at 8 A.M. and turned on at 4:30 P.M., for an indefinite period. It was with some difficulty that persons whose houses were not well furnished with window glass could discern surrounding objects with sufficient clearness to pursue their ordinary avocations. Much more so was this the case in the large stores where light was admitted only through the front windows and doubtful skylights, and in dingy offices, where the architects seemed to have endeavored to imitate the peculiar features of a Lapland hut in omitting windows altogether. "To show how necessary was this action, at a period when the supply of gas is short," said the press, "we may state that the quantity consumed on one day only amounted to 35,000 feet, and it is

Consumers' bills from the City Gas Works were not as low as the gas. *Confederate Museum.*

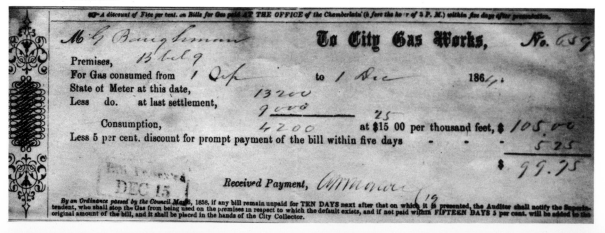

quite plain that if this had been allowed to continue for any length of time, it would have exhausted the resources, and placed our citizens entirely at the mercy of the candle sellers.

"Indeed, we regret to state that no sooner had the impression got abroad that the supply of gas was slowly, but surely, giving out, than the prices of candles commenced to advance; and housekeepers are even now considering whether it will not be well to invest all their surplus means in 'tallow dips,' ere there shall be from gas 'no light, but only darkness visible.' This is an illustration of the spirit of extortion which seems to have gotten possession of the very soul of men. There is no reason for the advance in the price of candles, and we advise the people against encouraging it by not making an unusual demand; for the danger of the gas supply becoming exhausted is unlikely. We learn from Mr. Fry, the Superintendent, that the defects in the Gas Works are nearly remedied by the construction of new retorts, so difficult to obtain until manufactured in the South, which are now on the way to Richmond. It may be proper to add that arrangements were made in August last for procuring these articles, but there was a delay in transporting them. They will be here in a day or two, and it is probable that even the inconvenience of having the gas turned off in the morning will last for a brief period only. We hope this statement will relieve the public mind, and remove the only plea for extortion in an article of household necessity."

While Richmond residents were reading the article, there was a terrific explosion in the city, and fire-alarm bells began to ring. One end of a building at the government laboratory had blown up, shattered windows in other buildings and houses in the neighborhood, and started a fire. In the rear of the establishment, which was known as the sea-coast ammunition room, men had been sitting in a corner, filling and ramming fuses. Probably from the fact that a vent was not properly secured, the foul air got between the drift and the composition, and caused the explosion.

Immediately after the explosion, fire burst from that part of the building, and men leaped from the shattered windows. Those who had been within a radius of some twelve feet of the explosion were very badly burned. Two of the men ran in flames to the river and plunged in, and another ran up the street with every particle of his clothes burned off. Workers who were able, and people who came running to help, grabbed buckets and used every water source nearby in efforts to control the flames. With so much ammunition, loaded bombs, shrapnel, boxes and kegs of woolen fuses, it was a miracle that the entire place did not blow up before the fire was finally extinguished. It was also amazing that no deaths occurred when many of the employees were so seriously injured. The government later constructed a building on the upper extremity of Brown's Island where all the work of driving fuses was carried on. But that did not end the explosions.

Little boys were throwing rocks again. The spirit of battle was rampant between these juvenile factions in different parts of the city. Playful imitations of the more serious engagements between the armies were getting beyond control. Youthful Mosby guerrillas were rising into gang notoriety, and all the demoralizing influences of war were developing on a small but ruinous scale. One of their recent rock skirmishes, vigorously carried on in the neighborhood of Howard's Grove, had led to the discharge of pistols. Union Hill had fought Church Hill and a boy in the first group had been seriously wounded when one of his own comrades fired the wrong way by mistake.

Sometimes idle soldiers from the hospitals went to watch and direct the tactics of the belligerents. The combatants often selected Sunday afternoons for these rock battles, although they did not confine themselves to any certain day or time. No one in authority seemed able to end the juvenile uprisings and the many physical injuries which resulted from such brutal exhibitions. Occasionally, however, the law took a hand. John W. Davis, a policeman, was in the lobby of the Spotswood Hotel when a rock came through the window. He ran out and captured three little

Alexander H. Stephens, Vice President of the Confederate States of America. *Confederate Museum.*

who had never seen snow, watched them in amazement and exclaimed, "I'll be hanged if that don't beat anything, riding on ice!" But the snow and ice upon the tracks delayed the trains, mail, and travelers, so the people grumbled. When it began to thaw, they grumbled too. Masses of snow came down on them from the housetops and some had their headgear crushed and their faces splattered with dirty water. Instead of rushing inward toward the wall of the house when they heard the rumbling of the avalanche, they obeyed a natural impulse and leaped for the street in time to get the blast head-on. The snow melted so rapidly that every thoroughfare became a surface of rich mellow mud through which horses waded and plunged, aggravated by the driver's whip. It was little better at the crossings, and if a man got over safely, he had the luxury of soiled and spattered pantaloons, and boots without a glint of luster. The ladies tried in vain to find a dry sidewalk, and many went home with damp stockings and muddy dresses.

The excessive bad weather and the consequent condition of the roads had caused a temporary cessation of all war activities. The vaunted Burnside expedition was a deadlock somewhere on the stormy coast and nothing of an exciting nature was expected from all the deep-laid schemes of the Yankees in that region. The President boasted that the world looked with astonishment and admiration upon the stern resistance the South had made so far, and that determination to open the spring campaign with even greater energy would see its highest hopes fulfilled.

The President did not mention General Lee, but the press noted that he was now in the mountain fastness of South Carolina with an army, in numbers and discipline, ready for any move the enemy might make. "The Veteran General is modest and unobtrusive to a fault, but we venture to say that the time will yet come when his superior abilities will be vindicated, both to his own renown and the glory of his country." Everyone was wondering what Mr. Jefferson Davis really intended to do about the popular General Robert E. Lee.

boys, one of whom confessed that he had thrown a piece of coal—not a rock. His mother, Mrs. Broughmeyer, said she had whipped him before and would do so every time she knew he had been throwing rocks. She also paid a fine of one dollar for her son's misbehavior.

Snow was pelting the city and sleigh bells were ringing. Youngsters were riding down the hillsides on their toboggans like a streak of lightning. A soldier from the deep South,

A thousand or more people gathered at the Capitol on February 18, 1862, to witness the termination of the Provisional Government and the inauguration of the permanent Government of the Confederate States in the convocation and organization of the new Congress. Long before the tap of the Speaker's gavel, the members-elect, the members of the Virginia Legislature, prominent citizens, several military officers, and many pretty ladies waited for the solemn and impressive ceremonies. Though spectators were packed elbow to elbow and were slightly annoyed by a delay in the proceedings, there were no unpleasant demonstrations.

The following Saturday, February 22 (Washington's birthday), Jefferson Davis and Alexander H. Stephens, President and Vice-President-elect of the new and permanent Government of the Confederate States, were inaugurated in Richmond. Although stormy clouds hovered above the city and the air was damp and chilly, downtown sidewalks were crammed with pedestrians (many of them new arrivals, there for the day only) and shouting souvenir vendors. Streets were jammed with vehicles of all descriptions, flanked by men, women, and boys on horseback. Flags waved from government buildings, business places, and private homes. Stores were closed, soldiers paraded, and

Residence of Vice President Stephens. *Valentine Museum.*

bands played. It was another great day for the people of the South, determined to win for the Confederacy a place among the nations of the world.

The arrangements made by a joint committee for the preservation of order successfully prevented any attempt to interfere with the regular program. At half-past eleven that morning, the two Houses of Congress met, and shortly afterward proceeded to the Hall of the House of Delegates of Virginia. A few minutes later, the President and Vice-President-elect, accompanied by the joint Committee of Arrangements, entered the Hall as the entire assembly arose to receive them. All other space was occupied by governors of the states, judges, and other distinguished guests, the gallery being reserved solely for ladies. Elsewhere in and about the Capitol, thousands of people waited eagerly to hear what the Chief Magistrate had to say in his inaugural address.

While the procession was forming under the direction of the Chief Marshal, Colonel Dimmock, and his aides, the President occupied the Speaker's chair in the House of Delegates, surrounded by the Vice-President-elect, the President of the Senate, and the Speaker of the House. At half-past twelve, they joined the procession which moved to the statue of Washington near the entrance of the Capitol. There a platform had been erected to accommodate all members of the government and those invited for the occasion.

The ceremony was opened with an eloquent and patriotic prayer by the Rt. Rev. John Johns, in which he earnestly invoked the protection of Heaven in the struggle of the Confederate States for independence. The President then stepped to the front of the platform and delivered his inaugural address, which was frequently interrupted by cheers and rounds of applause:

"Fellow citizens, on this, the birthday of a man most identified with the establishment of American independence, and beneath the monument erected to commemorate his heroic virtues and those of his compatriots, we have assembled to usher into existence the permanent Government of the Confederate States. Through the instrumentality, under the favor of Divine Providence, we hope to perpetuate the principles of our Revolutionary Fathers. The day, the memory, and the purpose, seem fitly associated. (Cheers)

"It is with mingled feelings of humility and pride that I appear to take, in the presence of the people and before high Heaven, the oath prescribed as a qualification for the exalted station to which the unanimous voice of the people has called me. . . .

"The first year in our history has been the most eventful in the annals of this Continent. A new Government has been established, and its machinery put into operation over an area exceeding seven hundred thousand square miles. The great principles upon which we have been willing to hazard everything that is dear to man, have made conquests for us which could never have been achieved by the sword. Our Confederacy has grown from six to thirteen states, and Maryland, already united to us by hallowed memories and material interests, will, I believe, when able to speak with unstifled voice, connect her destiny with the South. (Great applause) Our people have rallied with unexampled unanimity to the support of the great principles of constitutional government, with firm resolve to perpetuate by arms the rights which they could not peacefully secure. (Cheers) A million of men, it is estimated, are now standing in hostile array, and waging war along a frontier of thousands of miles; battles have been fought, sieges have been conducted, and, although the contest is not ended, and the tide for the moment is against us, the final result in our favor is not doubtful. . . ."

The entire address lasted about twenty minutes, and at its conclusion the oath was administered to the President by the Hon. J. D. Halyburton of Virginia, a Confederate judge. Thus was completed the organization of the new government, founded upon the devotion of a loyal and patriotic people, with the hope that all would work harmoniously for the best interests of the country.

One of the first acts of the President was a proclamation setting apart the following Friday as a "Day of Fasting, Humiliation, and Prayer before Almighty God for His protection and favor, that the country be saved from the enemy and from the hand of all who hate us!" The Confederates had reason to pray: Nashville, Tennessee, had just fallen into Federal hands.

The marble statue of Washington by Antoine Houdon in the Confederate Capitol at Richmond. *Virginia Historical Society.*

Looking east from the base of the Washington equestrian statue toward the Capitol. The crowd gathered here for the inaugural ceremonies. *Library of Congress.*

One reporter who had covered all the inaugural ceremonies, in and out of the Capitol, said it was impossible to go anywhere in Richmond without being pushed around or shoved out through a doorway into the street. Even in the streets, he complained, there was a lack of space for one more human being. "Any man or woman who was on our streets during the last few days, and took pains to observe squads of soldiers roaming about hoping to find shelter from the inclement weather, was soon convinced that the call for some well-known stopping place for them is most urgent and appeals to every charitable heart. We know not why the Government, whose officials must long ago have been convinced of this necessity, seeing, as they have, crowds detained here day after day to get their pay, has not long ago established a commodious and comfortable retreat.

"We almost envy the Yankee prisoners their snug quarters while we see so many of our brave soldiers exposed. The Army Committee of the Young Men's Christian Association deserves the thanks and assistance of the public in the enterprise which they have started on 10th street to meet the crying demand. Although their quarters have been in operation only a few days, hundreds have been refreshed and sheltered there; their accommodations, however, must soon be enlarged, for as soon as the existence of such a place becomes generally known among the numerous soldiers arriving here daily, they will be overrun.

"Other benevolent individuals may start similar establishments; they ought to be numerous, the expense will be mostly for lodging furniture, and the Government would probably supply this. The liberality of our citizens has been heavily taxed during the war, but is not exhausted, and they would help, to any reasonable extent, we are sure, in this matter. Their private doors, indeed, are often thrown open to stragglers from the street. We heard of one gentleman who recently took five or six soldiers home with him, and fed and lodged them. Hundreds are turned away from the hotels nightly and know not where to go. And often, we believe, the reception rooms at the hotels are filled with lodgers on the floor, anywhere just to be within doors."

Little was done for sheltering the soldiers, but the War Department seized all corn held for the purpose of distillation and the price of whiskey went up some 200 per cent. This had no influence on its consumption, however, and the number of barrooms in the city increased. There were also more unlicensed drinking places, closed by the police only to open again at some other hideout. Courts and prisons were filled with culprits accused of or sentenced for offenses and crimes caused by an overindulgence in liquor. The habit of soldiers on furlough or absent from posts of duty, and many civilians too, of wearing pistols and bowie knives was becoming more common each day. So many street and barroom fights and murders had occurred that Richmond was getting an undesirable reputation for rowdyism which its residents and authorities deplored. Liquor was blamed for most of the trouble and, under the headline DRUNKENNESS, the press said editorially:

"This vice is growing apace in the community, despite the very high price now asked for all kinds of stimulating fluids. Two-thirds at least of the offenses which the Mayor is called upon to take cognizance of are found to have originated in this pernicious practice. One of the most distressing sights in the world is to see men capable of maintaining themselves in positions of respectability sinking all, and blighting the reasonable hopes and aspirations of long years, in pursuit of the pleasure they hope to find at the bottom of the whiskey bottle. An old preacher, and in this instance a true one, has well said: 'A drunkard is the annoyance of modesty, the spoil of civility, the destruction of reason, the robber's agent, the alehouse's benefactor, his wife's sorrow, his children's trouble, his own shame, his neighbor's scoff, a walking swill bowl, the picture of a beast, the monster of a man.'"

At the Metropolitan Theatre another general row had started in the gallery, where a number of brazen women were surrounded by a crowd of drunken and unprincipled men. One man persisted in dangling his legs over the railing. Several persons in the audience pointed toward him and began shouting, "Put him out! Put him out!" At that moment a vocalist on the stage was singing "My Maryland" and many in the theater, thinking the shouts were intended for the vocalist, became violently excited. Oaths, curses, shrieks, and boos intermingled with the clash of knives and the discharge of pistols. Washington Jenkins, a policeman who tried to quiet the disturbance, was shot in the shoulder, and several in the audience were cut by knives. The turmoil in the gallery and the sudden panic and flight of the crowd in other parts of the theater made up a scene of rowdyism which caused the decent people to shudder.

"Such open violation of the law is without parallel in this community," exclaimed the press. "It is about time the strong arm of power was put forth to hold in check the spirit of lawless brutality now rampant in Richmond. It is time, too, that we should call things by their right names; for disguise it as we may, the city is infested with a gang of ruffians, whose presence, morally speaking, is much to be deprecated. The shameful practices of drunkards, libertines, and profligates, who have neither sensibility, honor, nor shame, are not natural to the South. The civil and military authorities should be competent enough to devise a scheme to strike at the very root of this evil and remove the temptations which allure the innocent as well as stimulate the wicked. If our citizens cannot be permitted to visit places of amusement or recreation, or even walk the streets at night, without the risk of interruption from these outcasts of civilization, then there might as well be no law; for law is no better than a farce unless sternly administered, especially in times like the present.

"The people have now become aware of the Cyprians, resident and accumulated, who have come to Richmond since the war, as well as the loose males of the most abandoned character from other parts of the Confederacy. They have been disporting themselves extensively on the sidewalks and in hacks, open carriages, et cetera, in the streets of Richmond, to the amazement of sober-sided citizens compelled to smell the odors which they exude, and witness the impudence and familiar vulgarity of many of the shame-faced of the prostitutes of both sexes. Smirks and smiles, winks, and, when occasion serves, remarks not of a choice kind, in a loud voice, denote the character of these immoral male and female solicitors. The Mayor, in answer to many complaints, having determined to enforce the vagrant law, has caused one lewd character—a female—to be taken up for obtruding herself in an obnoxious attitude before decent people. It is to be hoped that she will not be the only example."

One afternoon, an individual of foreign appearance pushed people aside on a downtown street as he rushed around a corner with several soldiers close on his heels, shouting "Stop that man!" They had pursued him for some distance when a fleet-footed policeman who had joined the chase collared him. A crowd collected and heard the soldiers identify the man as "a substitute who had received a handsome bonus to do someone else's fighting and, after deserting his company, was having a gay old time with the cash in hand." He was lodged in jail until he could be sent to the regiment from which he had deserted for the proper punishment.

The penalty of one thousand dollars or two years' imprisonment for harboring deserters did not perturb Mrs. Louise Langford. Detectives were sent to her house to look for one named J. H. A. Bowlar. "In her bed were two females who claimed to be very sick," said the reporter covering the story. "After a fruitless search about every part of the house, there was some doubt in their minds as to the truth of the statement made by the professed invalids. They returned to the room, insisted upon examining the bed, and found Bowlar under the two women. Getting wind of the approach of the detectives, the above-mentioned mode was adopted as the only one most likely to shield him from the law. The discovery, however, was a lucky one for Bowlar. When rescued from his hiding place, he was in a very exhausted state, and had he remained there much longer he might have suffocated. The women were taken to Castle Godwin prison to await trial. Bowlar spent a few days in jail at Castle Thunder, then was court-martialed, and sentenced to be drummed out of the service, and afterwards subscribed for another branch of the service."

The neighborhood of Seventeenth and Cary streets had such a bad reputation that decent citizens were afraid to pass that way. They were insulted, or their senses shocked, by the obscene conduct of persons loitering there. Houses were known to harbor many fugitives of the law and deserters from the army. One midnight the Provost Guard, one hundred twenty strong and under arms, commanded by Lieutenant Turner of the army, and the police under Marshal Alexander, surrounded the block of buildings and the alleyway. The police force then entered each house in detail. What some saw was reported as revolting. Eighty-nine persons were taken into custody. Every male in the block was arrested and confined in jail until the next morning, when a hearing was held by the Marshal. All opened liquor which was found was poured into the street, and unopened barrels were taken to the receiving store where receipts were given to the owners. Deserters who had been arrested were sent to their regiments, and shirkers from the militia turned over to the proper authorities. Many were provided with British Consul papers, and were released after being identified.

Civilians and soldiers, including Yankee prisoners, never ceased to break out of the old and ramshackled jails, and other buildings serving that purpose in Richmond. Sometimes their exit was on a wholesale basis. Mr. Hall, keeper of the city jail, and John Brooke, his assistant, were at breakfast when notified that some of the "fugacious rogues" were leaving without the jailers' knowledge or approval. Mr. Hall hastened with all speed to the rear of the jail and went into the room under the workhouse. There he found the lock broken on a grating leading to the street and two men about to escape by that route. One, Francis Osgood, had been lately consigned to the jail for committing a highway robbery, and the other, William N. Miller (a bogus volunteer "Colonel"), had succeeded in swindling two men out of seven hundred dollars by forgery and false representation. Osgood, a burly ruffian, surrendered quickly, but the doughty "Colonel" desired to go through at all hazards until brought to reason by a navy revolver. Nine other prisoners had crawled out before them and successfully dashed to freedom. Osgood and the "Colonel" were taken back to their cell where a hole in the wall, just large enough for the men to crawl through, was discovered. But they remained only a short time before making a more successful exit. In their final attempt, they broke the lock on the front door late at night and disappeared in the darkness.

General "Frustrated" Winder, as he was known in Richmond. *Confederate Museum.*

Prisons and jailers at Richmond, as sketched by James Gillette of the New York State Militia, a captured Yankee. *Harper's Weekly.*

Commanders in the army, too, were having trouble keeping their men in line. Deserters and delinquents were also being rounded up, punished, and hustled back to camps. A single regiment had notices in the newspapers warning a total of more than two hundred soldiers to report or be dealt with as the law directed.

Facing these conditions and a diminishing number in volunteer recruits, Governor Letcher called out 40,000 more men, and required all persons having valid excuses for not serving in the militia to appear and report them. A number were excused and some rejected. "We never saw so many ailments spring into existence in so short a time in our whole life," wrote a reporter. "Sundry men, who have heretofore been regarded as rivals of Jackson, and the American deer, for speed and endurance, have suddenly, but not unaccountably, fallen lame, and could be beaten,

108

apparently by a turtle, especially if the Board of Exemption happened to be the judges. Applicants urge all reasons that human ingenuity can frame to avoid duty as soldiers." But several stores on Broad and Main streets were closed with cards posted on their doors, reading, "Gone with the militia. Will return when the war is at an end. By order of John Letcher."

On March 1, 1862, President Davis, by authority of a secret act of the Confederate Congress passed the month before, declared martial law in the city and an area of ten miles around it, suspended the writ of habeas corpus, and appointed General John H. Winder to enforce the military rule. This failed to get the results intended, but some of the loafers, rowdies, thieves, and pickpockets did move to the outskirts of the city.

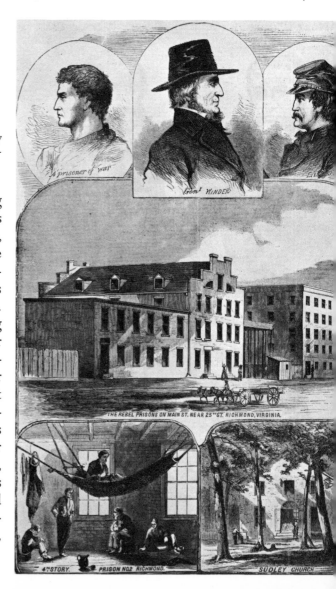

Soon Hollywood, Sidney, Shed Town, and Darby Town were being ruled by these "men about town," to the terror of all nervous ladies and young girls. It was unsafe for them to be out after sunset, or leave their doors unbarred. A lady of "veracity and respectability" said that a servant boy was knocked down, in broad daylight, on his way home from the post office with valuable letters for her, and unmercifully whipped by a set of suburban desperadoes. As the Provost Marshal's armed police were considered little better than the snoring night watch, heads of families on the outskirts of the city were advised to form Vigilance Committees for their own protection.

The host of undesirables in the Capital now employed clever lawyers to defend them. "Like other cities," said the press, "Richmond is not exempt from the presence of many pettifogging two-cent lawyers who glorify themselves in the courts by badgering decent witnesses to an insufferable degree while defending thugs still at liberty. Put all of these thugs and their lawyers in the front ranks of the army as dangerous weapons and the enemy will soon capture or kill them off!" But the Richmond lawyers were too influential for that; they went to work and, on April nineteenth, Congress materially modified the law under which General Winder had received such powers from the President.

The celebrated Negro pianist, Blind Tom, in later years. *Library of Congress.*

The only one who could not see what was going on in Richmond was the talented and celebrated Negro boy pianist, Blind Tom. The little wonder of the age, whose popularity was increasing as he grew older, was giving concerts at the African Church. He was playing to large audiences each night and the critics said he had greatly improved since his last appearance in the city.

The African Church, and some of its congregation, at Richmond. *Library of Congress.*

Complaints that all the Yankee Negroes were included in the number of abolition soldiers and noncommissioned officers sent North by flag of truce boats, were appearing in Richmond newspapers. That these representatives of the "irrepressible conflict" were returned "home" provoked much comment from Virginians and others "who had been robbed of their negroes and other property by Lincoln's minions." They recommended that these "black scoundrels" be sold and the proceeds applied to the paying of losses sustained by patriotic citizens who were fighting such "invading vandals." Some of the Negro captives, it was noted, would make excellent servants, and command, perhaps, $1,000 per head. To one editor, the confiscation of such contraband deserved, at least, a passing consideration from the authorities. Near his column, and headed PERSONAL, was a notice informing Thomas F. Sims that if he would call at the American Hotel he would find his slave Sammy, for whom a reward had been offered. Elsewhere, Clarkson & Company, 106 Main Street, advertised that persons having Negroes whom they wished to send to some safe place should apply to them for such service.

Enlistments in the Confederate navy, and contributions to a fund for the construction of gunboats, were accelerated by news of the spectacular battle between the ironclads *Monitor* and *Virginia* (*Merrimac*), the former of the Federal forces, the latter the hope of the Confederate navy. The battle in Hampton Roads, Virginia, had been exciting but ended in a draw. Nevertheless, it renewed the possibility, and frightened the Yankees, that the blockade might be broken.

"We are glad to learn that this example of naval warfare has set on foot a movement for the speedy completion of an ironclad gunboat of the most formidable character intended to put an end to the blockade maintained by the enemy," noted the press. "The success of the *Virginia* has given a wonderful impetus to this very proper enterprise, which will undoubtedly be pushed forward with all possible dispatch."

Another ingenious naval contrivance was also attracting the attention of Confederate leaders. It was claimed that the "machine" could be constructed for fifty dollars, and that a dozen of them placed in the channels of the James River would send the Yankee fleet to Davy Jones' locker in five minutes. The builder of the "machine" was Matthew Fontaine Maury, inventor of the torpedo, who was then living in Richmond.

The Ordnance Bureau requested the donation of all church bells which could be spared. The bells contained so much tin that 2,400 pounds of such metal, mixed with the proper quantity of copper, would make up a field battery of six pieces. The government gave a receipt for them with a promise to replace or pay for the bells at the end of the war. One of the first to respond was the Second Baptist Church. Its bell went into a field battery which, appropriately, called itself the Second Baptist Church Battery. A number of Napoleon guns, made from church bells and old French cannon long deposited at the Armory, were also being cast in the city. They were of brass, a third larger than the ordinary six-pounder, and were regarded as a most effective weapon.

General Lee had arrived in the Capital and had been appointed Commander-in-Chief of all the Confederate forces. Everyone agreed that he was the best general the South could have selected. There were objections that he was too cautious, but the same criticisms had been made against Washington, only to prove an advantage in the first revolution; possibly this would be so with Lee in the second revolution. It was argued that the most cautious general in the Federal ranks was Major General Don Carlos Buell, and he was the most successful. "General Lee," said the press, "is a man of great modesty of character, but of extraordinary energy, courage, and self-possession. In the early organization of our defenses in Virginia, he scarcely gave sleep to his eyes, yet so noiselessly and unostentatiously were his duties discharged, that no one knew, except by their results, what had been accomplished. The public never saw General Lee, but they saw the fact that lines of defense arose round their frontiers which, up to the present moment, have confined the enemy to Alexandria and Newport News, have held back his invading masses, and made his stereotyped cry of 'On to Richmond' the laughing stock of the world."

Spring weather brought people onto the streets, and what was termed the "bustling activity" of Richmond was evident. Everybody's carriage was out, and every merchant who had anything to sell found plenty of customers, no matter what the prices. Tempted by the spring sunshine, ladies made their appearance in the most stylish attire they could select or their means purchase. Soldiers were everywhere, some wearing flashy uniforms decorated with gilt cord and stars, others in more rusty garbs which showed they had been on the battlefields. March had come in like a lion but was going out like a lamb.

"The North has been making war upon the South for a year," noted the press. "It began the war at the wrong season—in the spring—although even then it promised itself entire success in sixty days. But the winter was the

Matthew Fontaine Maury, inventor of the torpedo, who lived in Richmond. *Valentine Museum.*

Drumming up recruits for the Confederate Army in front of the Exchange Hotel in Richmond. *Harper's Weekly.*

111

General Robert E. Lee on his favorite mount, "Traveler." *Virginia Historical Society*.

B-4858

period when it had all to hope for, and when we had most to dread. It had the whole spring and summer to make ready, to build its armadas, to discipline its hosts. It never doubted that by the end of the winter its power would be fairly established throughout the whole South. Its preparations and its efforts have been gigantic, its expenditures have been enormous. But the winter has come and gone, and the South remains as defiant as ever and indomitable. Even Virginia has not fallen in their hands. The city of Nashville is theirs, but they have met a Corinth. McClellan's enormous host is not yet in Richmond, which, if it fell into their hands would be a city of only forty thousand inhabitants, not the Southern Confederacy. A lion is in McClellan's path. He has changed his front from the Potomac to the Peninsula; he may have to change again before long. Meantime the spring has come; the burning sun of the South will soon spread havoc among the invaders of the South, and the diseases of the climate will prove more terrible than an army with banners."

It was not long until the guns were thundering above the battlefield of Shiloh. For days the two armies were tossed between victory and defeat. The Confederates under Beauregard and Johnston, and the Yankees under Grant, won on one day and lost on the other. But win or lose, each time the Louisiana troops charged the Yankee lines they cried,

"To hell with Butler!" Samuel B. Todd, a private in the New Orleans' Crescent Regiment, was killed, the press reported, "in defense of his country against the hireling invaders whom his sister's husband, Mr. Abraham Lincoln, sent to desolate our country and dishonor our people. It must be a pleasant reflection to Mrs. Lincoln, with her balls and soirees at the Federal Capital, that a gallant brother [he was a half-brother] should have thus fallen by the hands of her husband's mercenaries." It was also the last fight for General Albert Sidney Johnston, who was killed on the first day of the engagement. He was buried on the battlefield, but after the war his remains were removed to a final resting place at Austin, Texas.

A few days after Shiloh, reports told of the capture by the Federals of a locomotive called *General* and its recapture by the Confederates with the aid of another locomotive named *Texas*. At the same time, another locomotive arrived in Richmond which appropriately gained the name *Stubborn*. It was one of the larger locomotives and had been brought from Mr. Allen's plantation (Claremont) on the James River. It was now at the depot of the Richmond, Fredericksburg, and Potomac Railroad daring anyone to touch it. In the absence of steam, it was mounted on stout wheels and some thirty mules and horses attached to it. But this power failed to get *Stubborn* to its destination.

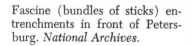

ing gabions (wicker frames with earth) for the defense Petersburg and Richmond. *onal Archives.*

Fascine (bundles of sticks) entrenchments in front of Petersburg. *National Archives.*

Confederate troops face a Yankee "Hornet's Nest" battery at Shiloh. *National Park Service.*

Near the corner of Main and Eighteenth streets, the traces parted and a dozen mules shot gaily forward, relieved of the iron monster, while the other animals were stuck fast to the pavement. An immense crowd gathered, and *Stubborn* afforded them considerable excitement for an hour or so. At length the team was properly hitched up again, but the combined horse and mule power, with the whips and "hi-hi's" of the drivers, availed nothing. Finally a strong rope was procured and made fast to *Stubborn* while some two hundred persons got in line to aid the quadrupeds with their labor. The experiment succeeded. With a long pull and a strong pull, *Stubborn* was dragged safely to the depot on Broad Street and set on the tracks.

Federal gunboats were more irritating than *Stubborn*—they opened an assault on Drewry's Bluff too close for Richmond residents to be comfortable. "Though late in commencing our preparations for defense of the approach to the city from the James river," reported the press, "the infernal gunboats of the enemy have been repelled. He went away, we have reason to hope, badly damaged after two

hours and one-half of fearful cannonading on our batteries. Our loss is slight, but another attack by the enemy certainly will be made. The proximity of their gunboats to this city places it in very great danger. Life, death, and wounds are nothing, if we are saved from the fate of a captured Capital, and a humiliated Confederacy. Let the Government act, let the people act, while there is yet time. If fate decrees the worst, let the ruins of Richmond be its most lasting monument."

The news sent many curious people to view the river defenses over the week end. Some of the men took rifles and provisions with them and offered their services as sharpshooters. Most reports of enemy gunboats which had been in circulation were found to be untrue. Nevertheless, Richmond residents continued to fear them. "Fortify the river," they cried. "What has been done? What is to be done? Why do we not have a complete system of defense against such attacks? Is it a matter of being everybody's business and nobody's business? To surrender Richmond would entail consequences that we fear to look at. Let the City Council give this subject their attention, especially those members who are practical business men, and have some brains, and know enough arithmetic to calculate the effect upon this city and its finances if an ascent of the James river is made by Federal gunboats!"

Richmond residents were also disturbed by what they were beginning to fear would be the annual summer appearance of Professor Lowe in his Yankee balloon. The "outfit" had again been seen about five o'clock one evening passing in the direction of the Meadow Bridge road. A report stated that "If it were as easy to puncture and let the gas out of these skyscraping-followers of Old Abe as it is to perform such an operation for those who remain on terra firma, there would be some comfort in seeing them going up. As it is, we are subject to the mortification of seeing them emulate the eagle, with the instincts of the buzzard. Not long since that distinguished aeronaut, Professor James C. Patton, of Petersburg, Va., came over to Richmond on purpose to proffer his services to the Government. After making several ineffectual attempts to reach General Johnston's headquarters, he gave up in despair and returned home. His services in extinguishing the Yankees by his intelligent observations of their whereabouts and numbers, would be of the greatest benefit if he were allowed an opportunity to come in competition with Lowe, the great gas-professor.

"We had a little target practice on one of the balloons opposite Mrs. Christian's farm yesterday afternoon. A superior rifle-gun had

"Flying Artillery—a hint to General McClellan which might aid his advance on Richmond." *Frank Leslie's Illustrated Newspaper.*

A Federal gunboat attempts to cut off a Confederate dispatch galley from reaching its objective. *Illustrated London News.*

the effect of making the Yankees draw down the balloon in a hurry. They conveyed it with rapidity to a point some distance off, when they sent it up again. Kemper's battery also fired a shot at the balloon. These little notices to quit may teach the enemy better manners."

A proclamation of Governor Letcher ordered all business places in Richmond, other than those engaged in filling State or Confederate contracts, to close each afternoon at two o'clock. This was done for the purpose of organizing a force for local defense, and to allow merchants and their employees the opportunity of perfecting themselves in military drill. The Governor's proclamation also called out the militia of the second class, who were required to meet daily in the Capitol Square for proper instruction.

"The Governor's move is a wise one," said the press, "and will obviate the necessity of all hubbub and humbug about raising a battalion for special service and to act as home guards. His Excellency deserves praise for putting down his foot firmly at the right time, on the proper subject in an appropriate way. The next few days will undoubtedly decide a struggle now going on near this city, and duty calls everyone to do all in his power to assist in that struggle. Let the people forego the pleasure of money-making for even a brief period and all will be well. We heartily hope to see an enthusiastic meeting this evening in Capitol Square, and a general turnout of all citizens able to bear arms." The Governor "put down his foot" just in time to hear the echo of distant cannon. Confederate and Federal forces were again at each other's throats.

Howlett's Battery on the James River blasts the Federal monitors and keeps them a safe distance from Richmond. *Illustrated London News.*

(Scene.—A Private Lunatic Asylum.)

KEEPER. "Yes, Sir; one of our incurables. Dangerous, you ask? No, not at all. Lately he has been rather *rabid*, but we keep him in check, as you see. Take Food? Yes, Sir, but sparingly: he has Strange Notions on that point, and no doubt has injured his brain by Eccentric Feeding. Noisy? Oh, very! sometimes makes such a Row that he disturbs all the other Patients. What are his Delusions, you say? Why, he has so many it's hard to remember 'em. Sometimes he fancies he's a General, and sometimes he thinks he's a Nigger; but oftenest he gets it into his head that he's a Newspaper Editor, which is the drollest of all—ha! ha! ha!"

GEN. McC———N. "Ah! indeed! Poor GREELEY! I heartily pity him!"

Harper's Weekly.

On to Richmond

The "On to Richmond" cry of the Yankees had started along the Williamsburg road before a general attack spread it out in all directions. On the last day of May, at Seven Pines, the battle for the city began in earnest between Confederate troops, under General Joseph Johnston, and those of the Federals, under General George B. McClellan. During a conference, Johnston fell asleep and had to be awakened to ask his opinion of a plan being debated. "Drive 'em into the river," growled Johnston. "Drive 'em into the river." The Yankees had crossed the Chickahominy at several points about twelve miles from Richmond on the previous day, and were attacked early the following morning by the Confederate forces. The fight continued until night, and the Yankees obstinately contested the ground from which they were repeatedly driven. The loss was heavy on both sides, and General Johnston was wounded so severely that he was unable to serve for several months. After a lull, the battle was renewed and continued as uninterruptedly as before. Both armies were reinforced, but Confederate troops never numbered more than half those of the enemy. As the Yankee advance was within sight of the spires and the sound of church bells of Richmond, Johnston made his counterstroke in the first grand battle of Eastern Virginia. By nightfall, he had driven the Yankees back toward the swamp they had crossed and taken about eight hundred prisoners.

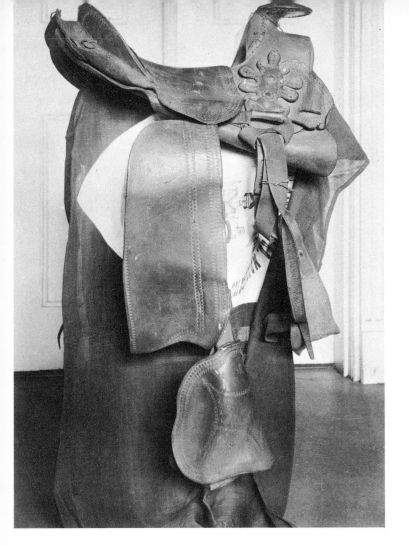

General Joseph E. Johnston's saddle from which he was thrown at the Battle of Seven Pines. *Confederate Museum.*

In this battle for the Southern Capital, every state in the Confederacy was represented. "One of the most interesting incidents of Saturday occurred with the Fourth North Carolina regiment," reported a Richmond war correspondent. "The color-bearer and his staff, being all killed and wounded early in the engagement, Major Grimes rushed to the front with the standard, and on foot bore it aloft through a perfect storm of shot, shell, and canister, and triumphantly placed it on the fieldwork, amid the cheers of his men. The regiment being (it is said) improperly supported, was obliged to retire, and did so in admirable order under a severe fire. When asked, 'How have you fared?' the stragglers and wounded almost invariably answered, 'Cut all to pieces! Cut all to pieces,' although two or three killed or wounded in men or horses covered the total."

Some of St. Paul's battalion, as they limped toward town shattered and wounded, drew the attention of the war correspondent. One

of them, who had been shot by a Yankee when in the act of drinking water, turned to him and quietly said: "Your gun is empty, you yellow cur, surrender or I'll finish you!" Having no inclination to be "finished," the Yankee gave himself up, and was handed over as a prisoner to proper hands. The Confederate soldier and other wounded comrades then regaled themselves on the roadside with cheese, butter, beef, and crackers extracted from the captured supplies of Federal troops. "Several hundred overcoats changed hands," said another soldier, "and I got one of them." Colonel Jenkins, Sixth South Carolina, acting Brigadier General, made a bold dash at the enemy with two regiments, capturing three pieces of artillery, a stand of colors, and spent the night in the enemy's camp, enjoying his rations and luxuries. But Patrick Kelley, of the Richmond Grays, had a narrow escape. A bullet struck a knife in his pocket, breaking off a portion of the handle and bending the whole. He sent both the bullet and the knife to his sweetheart.

Early in the action on Sunday, a continual stream of wounded lined the railroad, manfully trudging back to Richmond. Although composed of very young men for the most part, they bore their troubles and wounds philosophically, simply remarking, "The Yankees were running like the mischief when we left!"

"During the battle for Richmond," said a local reporter, "our city presented one of the grand spectacles which it is not often in the province of man to witness. The Capital of the State and of the Confederacy, environed by a hostile foe, whose thunder of artillery belched death amid our ranks, sweeping like 'chaff before the wind' our fathers, friends, brothers, husbands—yet there was no yielding heart, no quivering life, no drooping eye, even amid the thousand extravagant stories told by returning civilians, whose eyes are unaccustomed to the sight of battle's carnage; but every face wore that expression of intense

Confederate to captive Federal: "Come out of that coat." *Frank Leslie's Illustrated Newspaper.*

anxiety which betokened an iron determination to resist the ruthless tyrant's march, even till the last life shall be sacrificed upon the altar of our country's liberty.

"We do not believe that any city, since the world began, ever conducted itself with so much composure, so much calmness, so much quiet dignity. The prayers of all, of course, were for the success of our brave troops; but there was scarcely a man or a woman who had any doubt about it. They all reckoned upon their valor and patriotism, and they reckoned not in vain. A Yankee Colonel, who was captured and brought into Richmond, expressed his surprise at seeing such an enormous number of our troops dressed in Yankee overcoats. 'Every one came off a dead Yankee,' he was told by a soldier wearing one of them. We ourselves saw half a dozen splendid brass fieldpieces going up Main street last Monday, all marked U.S.A. (Uncle Sam's Artillery, we suppose), and all captured in the battles on Saturday and Sunday. For Lincoln's serfs to talk about beating us, when we have their

cannon, when we have thousands of their rifles and muskets, and their letters, and their portfolios, and have dressed a whole brigade in their overcoats, requires an amount of brass nobody but a Yankee ever had.

"Day and night, large numbers of gallant wounded were brought in and assigned to the various hospitals, and with mingled pride and pleasure, we witnessed the kind attention shown them by our citizens—some dressing wounds, some feeding the hungry, some with soothing cordials cooling parched lips, whilst ever present were those angel female forms, who, with saddened hearts but cheerful words, administered those little delicacies which revived in the soldier's breast that hopeful remembrance of their homes, in whose defense, so many have nobly fought and fallen. We would earnestly ask every mother and sister of Richmond to contribute their aid in alleviating the distress of our wounded, by contributions of cordials, bandages, cooked provisions, coffee, tea, et cetera, which can be sent to Messrs. Meade & Baker's or to the receiv-

Confederate soldiers after a battle "peeling" (stripping) Federal troops. "Sketched by an officer." *Harper's Weekly.*

ing hospital, at Seabrook's Warehouse, where they are much needed. We know the appeal will not be in vain; but let no one wait for her neighbor."

The sick and wounded had been arriving in the city since the first battle began. Hundreds of people came to the York River Railroad Depot with such conveyances as they had, or could obtain, loaded with mattresses, beds, and food for those arriving by that route. Others attended to taking down their names and regiments for the Inspector of Hospitals on Capitol Square. Even boys and girls came to keep the flies from disturbing the helpless soldiers by waving newspapers above their fevered brows. Many took refrigerators they could spare to the hospitals, and butchers collected all the beef and other kinds of bladders they had to be used as ice receptacles. Some women read to them or wrote letters to their families.

Five hundred Yankee prisoners also arrived that day and were marched off to the Confederate State Prison. "It is a sad commentary on the war," bemoaned the press, "to think that for the worthless carcass of each one of these vile scoundrels perhaps the life of a Southern patriot and gentleman was offered

up on the bloody altar which fanaticism and fiendish hate has reared in our land. They, each and all, deserve the halter as much as any thieves and murderers that have fallen victims to the majesty of an offended law."

While the sick and wounded were pouring into Richmond, various notices appeared in the newspapers: "WANTED — Information of R. E. Davis and Robt. Bailey, who were wounded on last Sabbath. They are members of Capt. Manney's company, Forty-first Virginia regiment. Any one knowing of their whereabouts will please report them to me today at No. 126 American Hotel, and relieve the anxiety of many friends. H. Bone. THE GENTLEMAN who loaned his Horse to an officer for the purpose of finding Surgeons for the wounded (during the fight on Saturday), can learn the whereabouts of his horse by note, addressed to Lieut. L. LINDSAY, Richmond Post Office. NOTICE TO HOSPITAL SURGEONS.—Any information about P. BOURGEOIS, (Saint Paul's Battalion Co. A), will be thankfully received by O. M. RENE, 1st Lt., Co. A, St. Paul's battalion, Address, Columbian Hotel, Room No. 45. WARREN MCMILLAN, a member of Capt. Flournoy's (now Capt. Roan's) company, Sixth regiment. Any information concerning him will be thankfully received by his uncle, Joseph McMillan, New's Ferry Post Office, Halifax county, or it may be addressed to WM. R. PUGH, Richmond."

On Monday, June 2, reports that movements along the whole Confederate line were of an uninteresting, desultory, and monotonous character, and that since the fierce combats of Saturday and Sunday little had transpired worthy of more than passing mention, brought relief to all the residents of Richmond. On that day, President Davis's message to the soldiers was read in all the camps:

"I render to you my grateful acknowledgements for the gallantry and good conduct you displayed in the battles of May 31st and June 1st, and with pride and pleasure recognize the steadiness and intrepidity with which you attacked the enemy in position, captured his advanced entrenchments, several batteries of artillery, and many standards, and everywhere drove him from the open field.

"At a part of your operations it was my fortune to be present. On no other occasion have I witnessed more of calmness and good order than you exhibited while advancing into the very jaws of death, and nothing could exceed the prowess with which you closed upon the enemy when a sheet of fire was blazing in your faces! In the renewed struggle in which you are on the eve of engaging, I ask

and can desire but a continuance of the same conduct which now attracts the admiration and pride of the loved ones you have left at home. You are fighting for all that is dearest to men; and, though opposed to a foe who disregards many of the usages of civilized war, your humanity to the wounded and the prisoners was the fit and crowning glory to your valor. Defenders of a just cause, may God have you in His holy keeping!

JEFFERSON DAVIS"

Directly beneath the President's address to the troops, as published by one Richmond newspaper, was this notice: "The gates of the Capitol Square having been opened during the night, and so fixed as to prevent their being shut, in order to allow cows to feed on the grass, notice is hereby given that any such animal found therein will be summarily disposed of, by being shot. By order of the Governor. Samuel Freeman, Supt. of Public Buildings."

The people did not have long to relax. The Yankees were still crying, "On to Richmond!" Near the end of June, newspapers flared with boldface headlines: OPENING OF THE GREAT BATTLE, HEAVY ENGAGEMENT ON THE LEFT OF OUR LINES, STORMING OF MECHANICSVILLE, THE FIGHT AT GAINES' MILL, SAVAGE STATION, FRAZIER'S FARM, MALVERN HILL, THE ENEMY IN RETREAT! The first blast of cannon had startled

The housetops of Richmond. *Valentine Museum.*

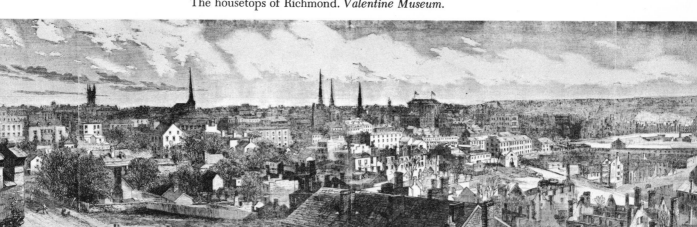

The President and Generals of the Confederate States of America. *Virginia Historical Society.*

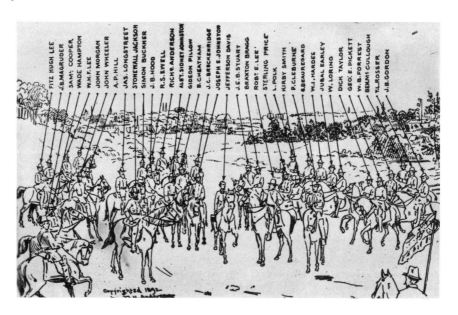

the city, unmindful then that for seven days the roar of battles would again echo above the housetops of Richmond.

Since the last Yankee drive to capture the city, General Lee had taken command of the Confederate forces in Virginia. He had planned and conducted the campaign which now set the Yankees galloping backward to more comfortable positions protected by Federal warships at Harrison Landing, on the James River some distance from the Capital. "Never was battle waged more auspiciously! Never was attack made with more bravery!" exclaimed the press. "The enemy was compelled to abandon their strong positions and leave them in the possession of our heroic volunteers!" The charge at bayonet point upon their powerful and entrenched batteries had been one of the most brilliant achievements in the conflict for the Capital. "Cut down the Yankee curs!" cried Confederate officers to their men as they dripped with their own blood and the blood of the enemy. Once more, the Yankees had been defeated in their bold attempt to take the city.

To answer the criticism in many minds that Lee had let the enemy slip out of his hands, one war correspondent wrote: "We think it a matter of regret that the public expectation was raised very high, at the beginning of the great effort to whip and eject the enemy from his position, as to the capturing of his whole force. The brilliant victory we have gained is overlooked by the sanguine expectation of the wholesale capture. And now that it is pretty well ascertained that the great body of the enemy's force has escaped, the triumph is measurably forgotten in the caviling at the failure to bag the whole concern."

"The victory is brilliant and complete without the capture," wrote another correspondent. "Our chivalrous army has driven from its fortifications, and ingloriously from the scene of its operations before Richmond, the most splendidly equipped, and best drilled and largest army ever organized on this continent. The disaster to that army is one of the severest, and the victory to our troops is glorious. There is too much to rejoice over to admit of repining that more had not been done!"

Before Richmond—the Battle of White Oak Swamp Bridge, June 30, 1862. The Confederates advance as Federals retreat across the river. *Frank Leslie's Illustrated Newspaper.*

Some war correspondents for Southern newspapers had expressed the fear that the siege of Richmond might last for six or twelve months, and that the Confederate strength in men and resources would be frittered away in dashes against the foe, which, though brilliant, would slowly but surely use up their endurance. "We trust that the result of the last two days' operations will stop all their croaking," said a Richmond reporter, "showing, as it did, that, when ready, our soldiers are able to march steadily on in the path of victory, a discomfitted and flying foe hastening before us. The Yankees have not yet got Richmond, but maybe, ere this paper reaches the distant reader, Richmond may have the Yankees. So mote it be."

Follow up the victory, demanded the press: "Fruitless, indeed, and barren will be the bold triumphs of the Confederate army before Richmond, if they are followed by a period of apathy such as that which succeeded the victory at Manassas. Now is the time for renewed energy and activity everywhere. The enemy must not be allowed to recover from the blow just dealt him with such stunning force. Let the cry be 'To arms! To arms!' Let the people rally to the cause with added enthusiasm—let the Government furnish the means and appliances of war with increased energy—and let the army move with more promptness and celerity than at any time since the war began. This is the way to put the speediest termination to the war, and the only way to win an early peace."

The President's words of thankfulness and encouragement to the army of Eastern Virginia were read to all the troops who had defended the Capital against another effort by the Yankees to capture it. With deep and sincere gratitude, he wrote:

Soldiers:—I congratulate you on the series of brilliant victories which, under the favor of Divine Providence, you have lately won, and as the President of the Confederate States, do heartily tender to you the thanks of the country, whose just cause you have so skillfully and heroically served. Ten days ago, an invading army, vastly superior to you in numbers and in the material of war, closely beleaguered your Capital and tauntingly proclaimed its speedy conquest; you marched to attack the enemy in his entrenchments; with well-directed movements and death-defying valor, you charged upon him in his strong positions, drove him from field to field over a distance of more than thirty-five miles, and, despite his reinforcements, compelled him to seek safety under the cover of his gunboats, where he now lies cowering before the army, so lately derided and threatened with entire subjugation. The fortitude with which you have borne toil and privation, the gallantry with which you have entered into each successive battle, must have been witnessed to be fully appreciated; but a grateful people will not fail to recognize you and to bear you in loved remembrance. Well may it be said of you that you have "done enough for glory;" but duty to a suffering country and to the cause of constitutional liberty, claims from you yet further effort. Let it be your pride to relax in nothing which can promote your future efficiency; your one great object being to drive the invader from your soil, and, carrying your standards beyond the outer boundaries of the Confederacy, to wring from an unscrupulous foe the recognition of your birthright and your independence.

JEFFERSON DAVIS

While the battles raged, the ever-recurring scenes were enacted in Richmond; trains brought in several thousand Yankee prisoners and many more than that number of Confederate wounded. Ambulances, ordered back from nearby battlefields, and other conveyances of all types carried the latter to hospitals; fathers, mothers, sisters, wives, and sweethearts waited—waited—waited.

For the past month, hospitals had been so crowded with visitors, some merely curious, that an order had been issued refusing admission to anyone not having a pass. No exception had been made for those related to patients, and this was angrily resented by one reporter, who, after many words decrying the practice, wrote: "We saw yesterday a lady who failed to have the necessary permit, begging to be allowed to enter Seabrook's Hospital to see a dying cousin. This was refused her, though she solicited it with tears in her eyes. When we last saw her, she was anxiously peering through the bars of the various windows, trying to discover the face of her dying relative." He also complained that, even though the neglect of the dead was sometimes unavoidable while taking care of the wounded, the body of a Confederate soldier had been left at the York River Railroad Depot for two days without the slightest effort having been made for its interment. "A blanket and an open platform is not exactly the sort of treatment our dead heroes should receive," added the reporter. Another item suggested that the numerous soldiers, straggling about the streets with nothing to do, and doing it bravely, assist in helping with things which had to be done.

As usual, after each battle, "Personals" giving the names of relatives or friends and asking that they get in touch with them or send word of their whereabouts, appeared in the newspapers. The eagerness for such information prompted the Secretary of War to establish the Army Intelligence Depot, which served that purpose until the hostilities ended.

That Fourth of July, many wagonloads of war material began rolling into Richmond from the nearby battlefields. Since the public had been warned of the penalty for collecting such "trophies," the government had employed teamsters, mostly Negroes, to do the work. The yield in guns, knives, clothing, and other articles was enormous. When a wagon came to a halt on the street, it was immediately surrounded by crowds curious to examine the relics. As large equipment, such as howitzers, cannon, caissons, and wagons marked "U.S.A.," passed by, the loot was greeted with loud cheers, sneers, and comments. Sometimes the purpose for which this material was made was achieved far from the battlefield. One Negro teamster, delivering muskets to the Thomas factory, had the fingers of his left hand blown off while attempting to pull one from under the load in his wagon.

"Since the series of battles around Richmond," a reporter observed, "the youths in certain parts of the city have been indulging in every species of sport resembling the sound and appearance of battle. Some of these juvenile would-be heroes broke open a caisson in the neighborhood of Twenty-first street, from which they extracted several pounds of powder, with which they prepared to give the denizens of the locality a salute. A hole was burrowed in an adjacent bank and the powder deposited, and innumerable brickbats piled upon it. A match was then applied, and an explosion resulted which would have laid the report of a twenty-four pounder in the shade. Should not the authorities stop the indulgence in such sport?"

The thousands of captured Yankees in Richmond, with prisons overflowing, forced the Confederates to arrange for an exchange of prisoners. On one day three thousand of them left Belle Isle prison, under a flag of truce, for Varina, the plantation of Albert Aiken, Esq., twelve miles from the city. There they met the United States army officers empowered to effect the exchange. The Yankee prisoners consisted wholly of soldiers; no commissioned officers were among them. The guard attending them was composed of a portion of the Forty-second Mississippi regiment, under a Colonel Miller. A guide from Captain Alexander's detective force piloted the party to the plantation. The Yankee prisoners were elated at the prospect of going home. On the way they were permitted to pass the Confederate States Military Prison at the corner of Twentieth and Cary streets, and, while in front of the building, they cheered their compatriots who were still in jail. The day was intensely hot, and after they had walked quite a distance, some of them collapsed and had to be left on the wayside, where a number died.

Six hundred other Yankee prisoners were sent from Richmond via the Petersburg railroad, to City Point, also under flag of truce, and were delivered into the hands of United States officers appointed to receive and convey them to the realms of Yankeedom. Of this number two hundred fifty were sent from the Confederate States Military Prison, most of whom were more or less wounded. Three hundred fifty of the men slightly wounded, or much debilitated by camp fever and other diseases, came from Belle Isle. Confederate officers said that when they went to the Isle and announced that a certain number of those most prostrated by sickness would be sent home, it was difficult to make a selection for, simultaneously, more than four thousand men were taken violently ill. Finally, the three hundred fifty who showed unmistakable evidence of physical suffering were chosen out of the large number of candidates. At this time forty-one hundred Yankee prisoners remained at Belle Isle, and another four hundred were at the Confederate States Military Prison in Richmond. The removal of the smaller group sent away was effected very quietly; only a few persons were on Cary Street when the long line of limping and disabled Yankees wended their way to the Petersburg depot.

The sudden spurt in the exchange program brought in and out of Richmond, between short intervals, twenty-five hundred Yankee prisoners from Lynchburg, most of them captured by Stonewall Jackson's army, and six hundred more from Salisbury, North Carolina. Among the latter were a Colonel Wilcox of the First Michigan regiment, captured at Manassas, who had been the first Yankee military Governor of Alexandria, Virginia, "a very affable and gentlemanly man"; a Lieutenant Hamblin, "son of old Tom, the play-actor"; and "the notorious Michael Corcoran, Colonel of the Sixty-ninth New York regiment." All were sent, by flag-of-truce boats, to City Point.

Another prisoner was Mrs. R. Frazier, "a Lincoln woman," who had been captured at the village of Whitehouse, not far from Richmond, after Federal troops retreated. She had stated that she had gone there to wait on Major General E. Sumner and several of her personal friends who were sick in that locality. Her colloquial power was said to have been most extensive. After being brought to Richmond and lodged in Castle Godwin Prison, the officers in charge respectfully asked to be relieved of her presence, "as the diarrhea of

words, not of the most choice kind, with which she constantly afflicted them was past human endurance." A Richmond reporter prophesied that the Southern people could confidently expect a dozen columns of twaddle about "experiences" in Dixie from this strong-minded disciple of Greeley. "Prior to her departure," he said, "she had the candor to acknowledge that she did not believe the South could ever be subjugated—a remark she confessed she had made to the Abolition General Sumner, which he answered by a look of incredulity. At an early hour in the morning, Mrs. Frazier was conveyed in a hack from the Castle Godwin to the C. S. Military Prison. Arriving there, she was requested to alight, but swore she would die first, as she had gotten in the carriage to go home, and did not intend to go anywhere else. In reply to her question, what building it was, she was informed that it was used as a receptacle for her countrymen. She then shook her fist with indignation at the disabled Yankees and yelled out to them that no Yankees would be in their present position had they fought like the rebels. Her remarks were deemed offensive by those to whom they were directed, and after the lady was carried among them, they contrived a plan to annoy her by getting up sundry letters to General Winder (an abomination to her eyes), requesting him to detain her in Richmond, as neither useful nor ornamental to them. The fact being communicated to her with becoming gravity by a Confederate officer, she then exhibited the first signs of being a woman, by shedding a few tears. She was finally made aware of the joke, and afterwards conducted herself more quietly, though she did rave and rant a great deal on being locked up in one of the ladies' cells."

It had been six weeks since the last gun was fired in battles around Richmond, and the press was complaining that a lethargy, as deep as that which pervaded the army and the country after Manassas, had settled down over them again. If so, they were aroused at the end of August by reports of another fight on that same battlefield, little more than a year later.

126

"Masterly Inactivity," or six months on the Potomac. *Frank Leslie's Illustrated Newspaper.*

General Lee had moved in that direction and planned a campaign which was to play havoc with the Yankees once more. The fight began in mid-afternoon, Generals T. J. (Stonewall) Jackson and James Longstreet forming their lines in a V-shape with the enemy between them. The Yankees made the first advance but were thrown back in great confusion. An artillery battery of twenty-eight pieces, commanded by Colonel S. D. Lee, mowed them down by the scores. When General John B. Hood's division advanced, and Jackson moved in, the Yankees found themselves attacked from all sides. The battle went on until after dark, when the Yankees were routed and pursued for three miles. They were so fast in getting away that Jackson, ordered to press them, replied that he could not catch up with them. Their forces had included the commands of Generals N. P. Banks, George B. McClellan, and John Pope.

Lieutenant General James Longstreet, C.S.A. *Cook Collection, Valentine Museum.*

127

One company of Confederates ran out of ammunition during the Second Battle of Bull Run and threw rocks at the Federal troops. *National Park Service.*

The loss of the Yankees in men exceeded that of the Confederates almost five to one. Their dead covered the field, and at Negro Robinson's house, their wounded were so thick on the floor that it was difficult to move without stepping on them. The Confederates captured numerous batteries, colors, and thousands of prisoners with all their guns and equipment. More small arms could have been collected but the soldiers didn't want to bother with them. Among the citizens from Washington who came out to see the fight, fifty were bagged by the Confederates and didn't get home for some time.

In Richmond everyone observed another day of fasting and prayer, for which the President gave his own words of thanksgiving: "Once more upon the plains of Manassas have our armies been blessed by the Lord of Hosts with a triumph over our enemies," he said. "It is my privilege to invite you once more to His footstool, not now in the garb of fasting

and sorrow, but with joy and gladness, to render thanks for the great mercies received at His hands. A few months since, and our enemies poured forth their invading legions upon our soil. They laid waste our fields, polluted our altars and violated the sanctity of our homes. Around our Capital they gathered their forces, and, with boastful threats, claimed it as already their prize. The brave troops which rallied to its defense have extinguished these vain hopes, and, under the guidance of the same Almighty hand, have scattered our enemies and driven them back in dismay. Uniting these defeated forces and the various armies, which had been ravaging our coasts with the army of invasion in Northern Virginia, our enemies have renewed their attempt to subjugate us at the very place where their first effort was defeated, and the vengeance of retributive justice has overtaken the entire host, in a second and complete overthrow.

Principal Confederate defenses near Manassas (Bull Run), showing the forts, breast-works, log barracks, and "Quaker guns" (large tree trunks set in place to resemble heavy artillery). *Frank Leslie's Illustrated Newspaper*.

Picking up debris after General Pope's retreat at the Second Battle of Bull Run. *National Archives*.

An artist taunts the idea of compromise in *Harper's Weekly*.

"To this signal success accorded to our arms in the East, has been graciously added another equally brilliant in the West. On the very day on which our forces were led to victory on the plains of Manassas in Virginia, the same Almighty arm assisted us in overcoming our enemies at Richmond, in Kentucky. Thus, at one and the same time, have the two great hostile armies been stricken down, and the wicked designs of our enemies set at naught.

"In such circumstances, it is meet and right that, as a people, we should bow down in adoring thankfulness to that gracious God who has been our bulwark and defense, and to offer unto Him that tribute of thanksgiving and praise. In His hand are the issues of all events, and to Him should we, in an especial manner, ascribe the honor of this great deliverance."

General Lee himself believed the Confederate victories were at a peak, and the opportunity to gain by peace what they had won by war was at hand. To President Davis he wrote:

Headquarters near Fredericktown, Md.,
September 8th, 1862.
His Excellency Jefferson Davis, President of the Confederate States, Richmond Va.

Mr. President: The present position of affairs, in my opinion, places it in the power of the Government of the Confederate States to propose with propriety to that of the United States the recognition of our independence. For more than a year both sections of the country have been devastated by hostilities which have brought sorrow and suffering upon thousands of homes without advancing the objects which our enemies proposed to themselves in beginning the contest. Such a proposition, coming from us at this time, could in no way be regarded as suing for peace; but, being made when it is in our power to inflict injury upon our adversary, would show conclusively to the world that our sole object is the establishment of our independence and the attainment of an honorable peace. The rejection of this offer would prove to the country that the responsibility of the continuance of the war does not rest upon us, but that the party in power in the United States elect to prosecute it for purposes of their own. The proposal of peace would enable the people of the United States to determine at their coming elections whether they will support those who favor a prolongation of the war or those who wish to bring it to a termination, which can be but productive of good to both parties without affecting the honor of either.

I have the honor to be, with great respect,
Your obedient servant,
R. E. Lee, General.

Within a few days, Lee invaded Maryland; the Federals were victorious at South Mountain, the Confederates captured Harpers

Ferry, and the battle of Antietam seemed to be a draw, with heavy losses on each side. Lee then recrossed the Potomac to Virginia, and in a report of his dispatches the press contrasted his proclamation to the people of Maryland with the despotic addresses of the Yankee commanders: "It places before Maryland a free choice of her destiny, leaving her at entire liberty, without menace or compulsion, to unite her fortunes with either the Northern or the Southern Union. In its spirit, its sentiments and language, it is worthy of the cause of Southern independence, of the great leader of the Southern armies, and of the magnanimous and heroic people whom he represents. General Lee, whose moderation, modesty, and unselfishness are as admirable as his resplendent military genius, will achieve for the Southern cause as much influence by the wisdom of his counsels as the prowess of his arms."

The Commander-in-Chief of the Confederate army was now regarded as one of the great military leaders of his time. His name, ex-

Commander in Chief of the Confederate Army, General Robert E. Lee. *Virginia Historical Society.*

ploits, and fame were lauded by everyone in the South. Not a day passed without some mention of him in the press. Probably the best description of him at this period of his career was written by a Richmond war correspondent. "You cannot imagine a plainer or more unostentatious looking man than the Commander-in-Chief of the Confederate armies—General Lee," he said. "Take a human form, say five feet eight inches in height, its constituents well knit together, full in its proportions, and yet without superfluity. Add to it a well-shaped, squarely built head, with a front whose every line is marked with energy and genius, a pair of keen, dark eyes —brown in the parlor, but black in the field— that seem to embrace everything at a glance; a handsomely shaped nose, such as Napoleon liked to see on his Generals; a mouth indicative of an iron will, and a countenance whose natural expression is one of gentleness and benevolence; cover the head, mouth, and lower part of the face with a heavy growth of short gray hair; invest the whole figure with grace, and an unassuming consciousness of strength, purpose, and position; let it speak to you in a voice whose tones of politeness never vary, whether uttered to the highest or the lowest in rank, and you have as full and com-

plete a description as I can give of the distinguished man who at this moment holds in the balance of his hand the destiny of his country."

Since Lee had assumed command, many things had been done for the benefit of the public service, and the soldier individually, which hitherto had been overlooked or neglected. The number of guards to and from camp were increased to prevent leave without proper permits, and the stragglers in cities or elsewhere, though still numerous enough, were made to realize that the penalty for such disobedience would be strictly imposed against them.

The Thanksgiving holidays gave Richmond people a short respite from fear of invading Yankees, but early in December the dread of another advance upon the city came from the direction of Fredericksburg, only a short distance away. Even the eventual defeat of Yankee General Ambrose E. Burnside on that Virginia battlefield did not wholly change their minds. "Whatever the Yankees may pretend hereafter," said the Richmond press, "it is evident that Burnside meant to make Fredericksburg the base for his operations in his advance upon Richmond. Even when Lee, with a powerful force, barred his way, he

A pictorial commentary upon General Lee's proclamation to the people of Maryland. *Harper's Weekly.*

Confederate troops at Marye's Heights, Fredericksburg, Maryland. *National Park Service.*

boasted that he was twenty miles closer to the Capital of the 'rebels' than was the main portion of the Confederate army. It is a high compliment to the sagacity of our commander that he so accurately predicted the designs of his adversary. Thwarted in this design, it is more than probable that Burnside will again 'change his base' and, embarking on the Yankee fleet in the Potomac, come down to the south side of the James river. Whichever way he may approach, we feel justified in saying that he will find us ready for him, as he found us at Fredericksburg."

Professor Lowe's Yankee balloon had been seen lolling above Fredericksburg late in the afternoon before the battle, and another reporter commented, "The idea of calling a balloonist a 'professor' could never have originated with anyone but a nation of humbugs. And the balloon itself, from a military point of view, seems to be as great a humbug as the 'professor.' On the eve of every battle, up goes his balloon, and at the close of every battle, down go the Yankees. It may be doubtful whether Lowe ever gets as high as the Yankee army gets low. The ascension of this Professor

of Gas to the heavens is an invariable signal for the descent of the Yankees to the shades. Lowe and his balloon, soaring in the skies, is an admirable emblem of the towering expectations of Yankeedom before a fight; the balloon descends, collapses, and is an image of their condition afterward. The Professor of Gas made a good many ascents in the Peninsula, and he made another on the eve of the battle of Fredericksburg. Long may he soar. He is the only Yankee who has ever yet been able to look down upon the Confederates. We may be consoled for that when we remember that he is the only Yankee who has yet exhibited a heavenward tendency during this war. If the blue empyrean can tolerate his presence, we can afford to let him soar over our heads like a buzzard, or some other obscene bird, especially when his appearance is always a signal of victory to our arms."

The Richmond press was amused by reports in Northern newspapers, which they never failed to obtain, that the Federal forces had occupied Fredericksburg with but little opposition until the rebel Lee and his army opened up on them with two hundred fifty

A cartoon in *Frank Leslie's Illustrated Newspaper* humorously depicts the President's southern tour.

The Overdue Bill
Mr. South to Mr. North: "Your Ninety Days' Promissory Note isn't taken up yet, Sirree!" *London Punch*.

He blunders upon the rebel lines, is fired upon by a picket, and displays his bravery.

His sketch of the affair.

His sketch of a battle, in which he is present in the "thickest of the fight."

The fact of the case.

His heroic exertions affect his health, and he gets permission to return home.

He brings home a cargo of trophies captured with his own sword.

How to report a battle—and live to tell the story.

pieces of artillery, while Major J. E. B. Stuart peppered their rear, and Burnside had to retreat because of overwhelming numbers. "Can't the Northern newspapers give some variety to their war whoops?" one reporter asked. "There is always the same disgusting sameness in their blood and thunder 'crushing the rebellion' articles. They bore us as much as their cannon. If the Yankees are going to devour us like roasted turkeys for their Christmas dinners, let them at least desist from hackling us to death with dull knives. We can put up with their rascality for it is unique, and, like the Devil, always keeps our imagination excited and expectations on tiptoe; but their stupidity is intolerable. Can't they invent some new lie, never yet uttered, against Jeff Davis and the Southern Confederacy, or a new war song, let us say, entitled, 'On To Richmond,' or 'Ten Days, Sixty Days, and Ninety?' "

One Yankee, however, did get to Richmond on a flag-of-truce boat. He had permission from both governments to travel on matters relating to the exchange of prisoners. It was his first visit to the city and at the wharf a Negro porter from one of the hotels said he would be glad to take the gentleman there. "What do they charge per day?" asked the Yankee. "Oh, sah," answered the Negro, "da don't charge by de day; dis hotel is run on de Ethiopian plan."

President Davis, accompanied by General Joseph E. Johnston, had left Richmond for a tour of the Southwest. They made stops at various places along the way, where the President spoke, hoping to encourage the people and the soldiers during the coming year in their fight for independence. He told the crowds that greeted him at Grenada, Mississippi, that if every man there of military age would join the Confederate army, all Yankee invaders would be driven back and across the Ohio River in short order. At Chattanooga, Tennessee, Johnston was asked to say a few words. He arose, looked over the audience, and blustered, "I would like to see all the men here, not wearing a uniform, in the army." The press reported his remark as "the shortest and the best speech since the war began."

At Murfreesboro, in the presence of Generals Johnston, Braxton Bragg, William J. Hardee, Leonidas Polk, Frank Cheatham, and John C. Breckinridge, the President reviewed the Confederate Army of the West. As he galloped on horseback along the lines of soldiers with the General of each division and his staff, regimental flags dipped, officers saluted, and bands played. It was one of the greatest displays of Confederate *might* during the War between the States.

Back in Richmond the scene was not so brilliant. At the Fredericksburg Railroad depot, a sorry spectacle was presented. Several flatcars, laden with wounded soldiers, were waiting for vehicles to carry them to the hospitals, and only about half a dozen citizens were there to take care of their needs. Many of them had eaten nothing since early the day before and were half famished, but very little food was on hand for them. They had all been drenched by rain during the night and, lying in their rags on the cars, hardly looked like human beings.

"This state of affairs is shameful," said the press, "and the Government should, in common humanity, take steps to have better management." Fortunately, someone at the depot got the owners of vehicles who were nearby to remove them before a large number of other sick and wounded began arriving from the Fredericksburg battlefield. A thousand Yankee prisoners, who also arrived at this time, did not present such problems. They carried their own sick and wounded to the hospitals assigned to them, and then marched off to Libby Prison and other quarters, where they were to spend Christmas.

A stout woman wearing a hoopskirt and a bonnet looked rather awkward in that attire to one of the provost guards at the depot. He spoke to her and was amazed by her deep voice and large hands. After a few questions, he discovered he was talking to a soldier who had not been granted holiday leave. He had put on the female disguise hoping to reach home without trouble and remain there for Christmas. The guard sent him back to Camp Lee where he was given picket duty on the front line for the next ninety days.

"This honored festival, the most ancient and the most universal, except Sunday, of the Christian World, again finds our country involved in the turmoil of war," read an editorial on Christmas day. "The rays of the rising Star of Bethlehem come to us through an atmosphere thick and murky with the smoke and gloom of battle, and the celestial anthem, 'Peace on earth, good will to man,' has a strange accompaniment in the clash of bayonets, the roar of cannon, and the demoniac yells and curses of foemen grappling each other in the death struggle of mortal hate.

"Yet long before the first Christmas that dawned upon the world, war has been the inevitable lot of our fallen race. No nation, nor tribe, nor continent, nor island, has been exempt from its ravages. The most dreadful of all the curses that Man's evil nature has brought upon the world, worse than famine and pestilence; and often bringing both in its train, it is still one of those calamities which we cannot expect to escape till the millennium dawns upon a regenerated humanity, and inaugurates the universal dominion of the Prince of Peace. In the records of Inspiration the existence, and even the lawfulness of war, in certain cases is recognized; but it is held up over the nations as a rod in the Almighty's hand for the punishment of the sins of man. The tendency of the spirit and principles of Christianity, undoubtedly, is to alleviate the horrors and ultimately to terminate the practice of war. But until the final triumph of that religion, the birthday of whose Divine Founder we celebrate today, we must submit to this, as to every other chastisement of the Almighty's hand, with patience and resignation, and perform with fidelity and courage all the duties which may devolve upon us.

"Christmas has ever been a day of peculiar festivity and enjoyment in the South, which has inherited the reverence of it from our Cavalier ancestry. It is a day which has brought joy to the mansion and the cottage, the master and the servant, and has never been dimmed by a cloud till the present unholy war. Alas! how many of our Christmas greens has the war blighted. Lo! many a chair stands vacant now around once happy firesides; how many a dirge of death belies the birthday of the Prince of Peace! But Hope, the hope of the Christian, can strike its roots even into the grave and put forth the blossoms of Immortality in the very gateway, through which Death has strode a conqueror. Let us have faith in God and in our cause and country. May the next Christmas smile upon a land from which the deluge of war has subsided, and the Dove of Peace return from the dreary waste to bring many a green leaf of beauty to our altars, and consolation to our hearts!"

Many residents, some with their holiday guests, went to the New Year's reception at the Governor's Mansion. Downtown stores and offices were open, and the weather favored those who had shopping to do, or arrangements to make for the coming year. All government buildings were closed, and the Mayor's courtroom was empty. Churches held services throughout the day and were well attended. But there was another affair of honor at The Springs on the Fredericksville road. Messrs. Harley and Rooester fought with horse pistols at twenty paces. At the first shot, Harley's pistol jammed, and Rooester missed his target. Their seconds refused to let them fire another round, and all returned to the city.

Theater and amusement places were filled to capacity that evening. A play titled *Jibbenalnossy* was the bill at the Richmond Varieties, with Clementine DeBar in the cast. It concluded with the afterpiece *P. P.* or *Man and Tiger*. Harry Macarthy and Miss Lottie Estelle filled the Broad Street Theatre with their songs, dances, new anecdotes, and banjo solos. At Shad's Hall there was a Grand Ball for gentlemen who had two dollars, and their ladies.

Sculptor A. Galt opened an exhibition at his studio to show the public his busts of Southern notables, among them Jefferson Davis, Governor Letcher, and Stonewall Jackson. He was very proud of a large head representing the genius of the Confederate States, which he had just finished. Shortly after the

Popular songs of the Confederacy during the War. *Library of Congress.*

exhibition, his untimely death from smallpox took from the city a talented artist.

In mid-January, the President returned to the Capital and was greeted at the Southern depot by a cheering crowd. Mr. Davis was in excellent health and fine voice. He spoke briefly, saying that prospects for the victory of the Confederate arms in the Southwest, which he had just visited, was assured.

At the Executive Mansion, several hundred cheering persons assembled, with Smith's Band, to serenade Mr. Davis. After the band had played two popular airs, he appeared at the door and gratefully thanked them for the manifestation of their regard and expressed his pleasure at meeting them again on his return to the Capital. He spoke of the Confederate States as a Commonwealth and the theater of the bloodiest battles of two revolutions in defense of the principles of liberty. Now, he believed, the incentive to fight was even stronger than when their forefathers threw off the yoke of tyranny, for they had had an open and manly foe while the enemies of the Confederacy came as savages and murderers, despoiling the homes of the living and the graves of the dead. Any further association with Yankees was looked upon with loathing and horror, said the President, and even the companionship of hyenas could be more readily tolerated by the people of the South. He spoke of the recent victories of the Confederate armies as having caused the brightest sunshine to fall upon their cause. One year ago, he said, many citizens were despondent; but now mark the difference—the gallant Lee, who largely shared the noble characteristics of his father, "Light Horse Harry" of the revolution, had repeatedly driven back the invaders of Southern soil; and recently, when they gathered for their mightiest effort at Fredericksburg, they were again hurled back and suddenly stopped in their movement "On to Richmond." Some of them did come to Richmond, and, he hoped, every battle would bring a few more of their disarmed and discomforted heroes, prisoners, and conquerors. So, too, in the West, at Murfreesboro, another brilliant achievement had just been won, and at Vicksburg the enemy was thwarted in its gigantic project for opening

C. R. M. Pohlé, the celebrated Drum-Major of the 1st Regiment of Virginia Volunteers. *Confederate Museum.*

the navigation of the Mississippi. This he believed would dampen the ardor of the people of the Northwest, to whom the Mississippi river was indispensable as an outlet of trade, and he predicted the most beneficial effects for the Confederacy from it. The present, however, was no time for the people to relax their efforts. If the enemy on every front were met with flashing courage and resolution, Confederate troops would be victorious, and, in time, conquer a lasting peace. The resources of the South, developed during the war, had astonished the world, he said, and he believed they would continue to increase so long as they were engaged in hostilities.

The President paid a high compliment to the women of Virginia, which was appreciated by those in the crowd. He spoke of the women, representing every state in the Confederacy, whose devotion to the sick and wounded soldiers had given them courage to fight again. With such women at home and such soldiers in the field, the eventual success of the Southern cause was inevitable. He spoke of the pleasure it would give him to mingle socially with the people of Richmond, but the cares and anxieties of his position left little leisure for the indulgence of the finer feelings of his nature. In days to come, however, when Southern independence was achieved and the Angel of Peace spread her bright wings over the land, it would be delightful to see more of his friends to whom he was indebted for so many acts of kindness. At the close of his remarks, the President invoked the blessing of God upon all people throughout the South, and bade his audience good night. After he retired, the band performed a few more pieces, and the crowd departed, their spirits brightened by the heartening words of their leader.

The Richmond press commented on Lincoln's Emancipation Proclamation, which had just been issued, and said that the South had given him an answer at Fredericksburg and Murfreesboro. In the same newspaper was a notice reading: "FREE NEGROES FOR SALE AT AUCTION. In pursuance of an order of the Hustings Court of the City of Richmond, made at the December term of said Court, I will sell on MONDAY, the 11th of January, 1863 (that

Captain Sally Tompkins was the only woman commissioned in the Confederate Army. She conducted the Robertson Hospital in Richmond at her own expense. *Confederate Museum.*

being Court day), in front of the City Hall, to the highest bidder, for each, the following Free Negroes, convicted of grand larceny, and ordered to be sold into absolute slavery, viz: Sarah Edmonson, Edward Patterson, and Nathan Drayton. Sale at 10½ o'clock A.M., Thos. O. Dudley, Sergeant of the City of Richmond."

It also published the following under RUN-AWAYS: "TWO HUNDRED DOLLARS REWARD. Ran away in the month of August, 1862, my negro woman, LISA, sometimes called ELIZABETH, half white, hair inclined to curl, large black eyes, tall and straight, a small spot on one side of her face, does not speak very quick when spoken to, about 18 or 20 years old, was formerly owned and sold by Mr. Lipsonan, living at Brook Rock in the County of Chesterfield. She may be lurking about in that vicinity, or the town of Manchester, or the City of Richmond, about which place she is well acquainted. The above reward of $200 will be paid for her delivery to me at the Public Warehouse, or secured in any jail so that I can get her again. B. J. Vaughan, Richmond."

A proclamation by the Governor during the first month of the New Year required male citizens between the ages of forty and forty-five, not exempt by the laws of the state from military service, to enlist immediately for a period of six months unless sooner discharged. They were to be trained and aid the militia in repelling any attempt to invade the city. Employees of transportation and communication agencies, banks, and others whose civil duties were necessary in carrying on the war were among those exempted.

Following publication of the order, military authorities were unusually active in rounding up all the delinquents who had not complied with the provisions of the Conscript Act.

140

Those not having the necessary documents (exemption papers and so forth) were taken in custody by the proper officers and hustled off to Camp Lee, where they were instructed in the rudiments of military art. Corralling these delinquents became such a problem that the Richmond Light Infantry Blues, of which the city was very proud, were assigned to aid the Provost Guard. It was their duty to make the people sensible of the obligations they owed their country in their war for independence, and they took care of the matter exceedingly well. If a man's credentials did not pass muster with them, they got a little rough.

Camp Lee was considered a "grand receptacle" for all sorts of recruits, conscripts, and paroled prisoners. Since the men were from all the states and every branch of the service, it was difficult to keep discipline. Fights, smashing windows, breaking furniture, and other disorderly conduct were everyday affairs. The arrival of new men at the moment guards were called elsewhere to quell such riots often gave those just brought in an opportunity to disappear again. Some had escaped and been dragged back to the camp a number of times. One of these, after being "repeatedly rounded up," had a brilliant idea. If he could not get out of the service one way, he would try another. Fearing he would pass the physical examination, he took a fit and wallowed in the dirt until a doctor was called. The doctor pronounced him healthy in every respect and the conscript was "hustled" into training.

If the press meant to encourage enlistments, newspapers went about it in an indirect way. "Unless we meet some great and unexpected disaster," said an editorial, "the war must virtually be ended by the first of June. The ascendency of the Democratic party in the North; their partial failure of the draft, and the entire cessation of the volunteer call; the admission by them that a large part of their army goes out of service in May, and that no new recruits can be had to take their places; the frequent and numerous desertions from the Federal army, their domestic dissentions; their bitter denunciations of Lincoln, his Cabinet, the Abolitionists and all New England; the imminence of national bankruptcy; the ruin of their shipping and commercial interests, and incipient social anarchy, all prove that they can keep up the war but a few months longer. Everyone who wants to have a hand in our glorious victory should enlist at once, or else an early peace may deprive him of the opportunity of helping to win the independence of the South."

Too much of the rushing that was done came from the inside to get out, rather than the outside to get in. Deserters and citizens avoiding the call to duty continued to fill jails and old buildings unfitted for imprisonment—from which they scrambled at every opportunity. Some were taken out to be shot, some were shot while trying to get out. There were day-to-day reports of such incidents in all Richmond newspapers. "The City Jail is certainly the most unsafe prison to be found in the entire Commonwealth, and will have to be rebuilt, or very much strengthened, if prisoners are to be held in it," noted one. "It

President Davis defies the intruders soaring above his slaves. *Library of Congress.*

Castle Thunder Prison, Richmond; S. R. O. (standing room only). *Library of Congress.*

is so completely jammed with all sorts of criminals that neither the Mayor nor the Courts know what to do with them." Another reported that the State prison was also overflowing with convicts of every grade and description, and that the worthy superintendent had great difficulty in keeping any kind of order there. "Unless the next Legislature makes some disposition of these creatures the prison will have to be greatly enlarged," said that report.

The appropriately named Castle Thunder prison had just been relieved of several inmates, one having been captured after being shot in the shoulder. Those who escaped had removed a large stovepipe which passed through the floor of their room, and, crawling through the hole to a basement, easily made their exit. The "honor guest" there, however, made no attempt to "dispense with the prison facilities." He was Moses Overton, General Lee's bodyguard, serving time for desertion, knowing how lucky he was not to have been shot. Several others at Castle Thunder, under sentence of death for desertion, were awaiting the date for their execution; thirty more, just committed on the same charge, were facing similar verdicts. At Libby Prison, two Yankee officers were about to draw lots to see which would be hanged in retaliation for an order by General Burnside that a Confederate

recruiting officer be strung up on a rope until dead.

The "winter colony of jail-birds," who had served short sentences, were again enjoying the good weather and sunshine of the approaching summer. Their innocent countenances and nimble fingers were exploring shops, auction rooms, theaters, and all other places of public interest. With ripe fruit on the trees and flowers blooming everywhere, they were picking the pockets of unsuspecting victims. At an auction of a billy goat, where "the bidding of the useless animal was spirited, and at last reached the extraordinary figure of $1,030, at which price it was cried out to Mr. Samuel Moon, Commissioner of the Revenue," pickpockets decided that money was too plentiful and went to work. Five persons, interested in the goat, were fleeced of their wallets.

Rank, dignity, or persons of importance made no difference to them. Generals, soldiers, statesmen, and government employees, no matter who or what, all were having their pockets picked. It seemed only the Mayor was overlooked. Even the churches called upon the police to be present at services, for pickpockets were operating there. "Every good citizen should deem himself a special policeman to look after the scores of thieves and pickpockets now infesting Richmond," warned the press. "However vigilant the police, they cannot be everywhere, the thieves soon know them and shun them; but private citizens may readily detect many of them, and they ought to do so. Putting them on the chain gang might solve the problem to some extent. They are as lazy as a negro, and no better, and for a lazy person, work is punishment." Had prisons not been so full, probably something would have been done with the "profession," but they went merrily on their way most of the summer. Their number always diminished when winter set in and they "took up their residence with the law as protection against the inclement weather."

With all good intentions, the City Council adopted a resolution to remove all soldiers and other prisoners confined in the City Jail for offense against the Confederate States, since they produced all the rowdyism which made the place so famous in the local annals. But what was done with them, reports failed to disclose. The Council also passed a city tax bill for the support of the municipal government. It listed a personal tax ("slaves, $1.25 on each $100 value"); a head tax on white persons of four dollars each, and of slaves, five dollars each; taxes on real estate, money, credit, bankers, brokers, manufacturers, keepers of ordinaries (barrooms and taverns); keepers of Negro jails and agents for selling and hiring out slaves; dealers in horses, mules, and horned cattle; auctioneers; transportation and telegraph companies with offices in Richmond; and a long list of various trades, divided into classes. No free human being escaped the tax; death and the undertaker paid too.

Congress was still in session, and the Custodian of Capitol Square had put up the usual summer notices, KEEP OFF THE GRASS. The city's Niagara sprinkler was ready for operation should streets become dusty and high winds threaten to fill the eyes of citizens— and every nook of their homes—with the whirling earth. The people prided themselves on having established, after two years of war, factories to produce articles formerly made only in the North: hats, shoes, oilcloths, percussion caps, chemicals, medicines, castor and

linseed oils, printing and writing ink, guns, knives, swords, files, saws, axes, hammers, brooms, brushes, perfumery, fancy soaps, glue, and scores of other articles which the Yankees had once poured into the South by cargoes and grown rich on their sales. All of these were now manufactured and sold by Richmond citizens, to the benefit of the entire South and the success of the Confederate arms, boasted the press.

"Some of the most beautiful bonnets that we have seen this summer were made of rye straw, or crochet of linen and cotton thread, by the ladies of Richmond and its vicinity," said one reporter. "These bonnets are neatly trimmed, and because they exhibit an independence on the part of the ladies that must be commended by every patriot, they are vastly more becoming than any Yankee trash ever brought to this city. Every lady who wishes to do so, can easily learn the art of braiding straw and crocheting thread, and may thus, at very little cost, secure for herself a beautiful headdress. We understand that one of our enterprising citizens has employed a number of ladies to braid straw, and that he is about establishing a hat and bonnet factory, from which to supply the wants of our community."

One of the largest and most important of all establishments in the South for producing war supplies suffered another great catastrophe at this time. A dreadful explosion at the government laboratory on Brown's Island, where ammunition was handled, destroyed part of the property and killed thirty-three employees. It was caused by the ignition of a friction-cannon primer in a room used for breaking up condemned cartridges. Hardly anyone in that part of the building escaped injury when the accident occurred.

Many of the female victims were horribly burned about the body by the exploding powder and the inflammable material of their dresses, which caught fire immediately. Some poor creatures who were able to rescue themselves from the debris ran about the island with their clothes in flames, shrieking for help. One, frantic and blazing, ran toward a storehouse which contained enough combustibles to have rent in fragments every tenement on the island, had it exploded. She was seized by several workmen just in time to bar her entrance. The damage prevented work at the laboratory from being resumed for more than a week.

Two fire engines, ordered for the city several years before, were delivered just in time to be of real service. They had been manufactured by Messrs. Ettenger and Edmond, of Richmond; one was bought by the Common Council, and the other was a gift of the insurance companies. The engines were given a tryout on the Basin bank where they were stationed. Their capacities were found to be nearly the same, although the advantage was slightly in favor of the later model presented by the insurance companies. Both worked admirably, and threw more water with greater force than the old hand engines operated by a regiment of men. After acceptance by the city, they were taken to Tenth Street to be ready for any emergency. It was believed that the city was now well protected against the efforts of incendiaries. Within a few weeks, however, fires destroyed much government, state, and private property.

The first occurred at the public warehouse, known as Brown's Addition, fronting on Canal Street opposite the packet landing. The entire building and its contents went up in flames, but property surrounding it was saved. The

most serious of all was the burning of the Crenshaw Woolen Mills and a part of the Tredegar Iron Works, which adjoined it. The fire started at two o'clock one morning, and the press described it as "the most destructive and disastrous conflagration which the city had ever been called upon to suffer." It originated and was first discovered in the picking room of the Crenshaw Woolen Mills, situated on the canal, and although it had made but little headway when discovered, such was the combustible nature of the material in the room that the flames spread with a rapidity that soon enveloped the whole building, and prevented anything from being rescued. The splendid machinery of the factory, the loss of which, at that time, was irreparable, was involved in the ruins, besides a heavy stock of material used in the manufacture of cloths. This material included over 30,000 pounds of wool, in the various stages of preparation for manufacturing purposes. In addition, there were in the building, destroyed with everything else, some forty pieces of finished goods, double width, amounting in all to about one thousand yards, and some three to four thousand yards of the same goods, woven but not completed.

The mill was one of the most extensive and valuable for the production of woolen goods in the Confederacy, and its loss seriously limited the supply of these essentials. Since

Type of fire engines supplied by Ettenger and Edmond of Richmond. *Valentine Museum.*

A passenger boat at the packet landing on the Kanawha Canal. *Frank Leslie's Illustrated Newspaper.*

The Tredegar Iron Works (left) and Crenshaw Woolen Mills (right) which suffered a great loss by fire at a time when their products were most needed by the Confederacy. *Virginia Historical Society.*

the beginning of the war, it had been turning out large amounts of serviceable cloths for soldiers, and finer materials for citizens' wear and officers' uniforms. At the time of its destruction it was making about two thousand yards of double-width goods per week, with a capacity to manufacture annually goods sufficient to clothe from forty to fifty thousand men. About one hundred fifty operatives were thrown out of employment by the disaster, and an estimated loss of $250,000 was sustained on the building, machinery, and stock.

From the woolen mill the fire rapidly spread to the valuable Tredegar Iron Works, and before the flames were under control the machine, boring, pattern, blacksmith, and carpenter shops of that establishment were destroyed. There were many heavy guns on hand, ready for service, which fortunately, received little or no injury. A large force of men immediately went to work clearing away the rubbish and covering the machinery left in the open when buildings were destroyed. The loss to the proprietors was very heavy, and the delay in the manufacture of guns to some extent handicapped the war effort of the government, but within a few weeks all the Tredegar shops had resumed operations. The conjecture was general that the fire was the result of incendiarism.

Confederates raid a train carrying Yankee troops. *National Archives.*

While these fires were burning, some Yankees were tearing up the tracks of the Central Railroad a short distance above the city. Informed of what was happening, several employees of the railroad climbed aboard an engine named *Augusta* and proceeded in that direction to get the facts. When they arrived at Peake's, about seven miles above Richmond, they discovered the Yankees and the Yankees discovered them. The employees barely had time to run for the woods when the Yankees descended upon the engine and took possession of it. With a full head of steam, they started off with *Augusta,* not knowing that the supports of the bridge over Chickahominy swamp were old and needed to be replaced. When they reached the bridge it slowly descended, taking *Augusta* and the Yankees with it. The Yankees then abandoned *Augusta* and disappeared. When the employees returned, *Augusta* was sticking up in the mud with nothing but the smokestack damaged. The engine was later brought back to Richmond, repaired, and put into further service.

The summer months were expected to bring some relief to Richmond in the matter of food supplies, which were becoming more and

A typical high, wobbly railroad trestle outside Richmond. *National Park Service.*

more limited, and prices were remaining enormously high. "We cannot believe that provisions are so scarce that the community must suffer for a want of its daily needs," noted the press. "The system of transportation is either obstructed or insufficient to do the work. The Government has forestalled this market by shifting commodities in transit to other than direct routes to our city to keep the latter open for its own use. Alarmed by the seizure of certain supplies by the Government when they arrive here, many companies, formerly sending them to Richmond, have discontinued doing so. This is especially true in regard to meats and bread stuffs.

"All these excuses, operating together, have perilously diminished the supplies for our city. So great has been the falling off of almost everything we need, that it is now a serious question for consideration of both the Government and the people. Richmond is the Capital of the State and of the Confederacy. A large part of its population is engaged in the service of both governments. Their duties are here, and here they must remain.

"Then there are large numbers of people employed in various other kinds of government work, such as arms and machinery. Some are providing food and lodging for all the rest, including those who only sojourn here while looking after certain government affairs. With all this there are still the hospitals, and their numerous attendants—physicians, nurses, stewards, and others taking care of sick and wounded soldiers. So that we find an immense surplus population here, forming a great city in itself, separate and apart from our own Richmond of former years, which requires a vast amount of provisions. The people are already hard pressed by the scarcity of necessities and the exorbitant prices, and there is reason to fear that the problem is yet to be heavier, unless something is done to allow their needs to flow more freely into the city. So far as extortioners are concerned, our generals can do no better service to the country than to seize all of them. They know how to charge! Put them in the army! Give them bayonets, and let them *charge* the enemy!"

The President, in his message to Congress in mid-April, confessed that all the people of the South must produce more supplies of food and meats than of cotton and tobacco if they and their armies were to win the war. As he had so often said, he reminded them, the war was to be a long war, and the only condition offered for peace by the enemy was that of subjugation. "We have reached the close of the second year of the war, and may point with just pride to the history of our young Confederacy," declared Mr. Davis. "Alone, unaided, we have met the most formidable combination of naval and military armaments that the lust of conquest ever gathered together. Let us all unite in the performance of our duty, each in his sphere, and with concerted, persistent, and well-directed effort, there seems to be little reason to doubt that, under the blessing of Him to whom we look for guidance, we will maintain the sovereignty and independence of these Confederate States, and transmit to our posterity the heritage bequeathed to us by our fathers."

Richmond was thrown into a high state of excitement by reports of a Yankee raid at a railroad station only eight miles from the city. A company of volunteer cavalry (about one hundred men) started out from Richmond in search of the raiders. The cavalry, galloping about in the rural districts and asking for information of them, so frightened the farmers that for several days they refused to bring in any produce to the city's markets. After the

The Great "Cannon Game"
Abe Lincoln (aside): "Darn'd if he ain't scored ag'in! Wish I could make a few *winning* hazards for a change." *London Punch.*

cavalry returned, having failed to run down the raiders, the farmers resumed their usual visits to the city.

"The campaign of 1863 has begun," said the press, "and the demonstrations by Hooker's raiders near Fredericksburg, shows that it will be an active one." General Joseph Hooker had replaced Burnside as commander of the Potomac army, and now faced Lee on the same battleground. While the fighting was going on there, other divisions of the Federal army moved against Lee from the opposite direction, which brought on the battle of Chancellorsville, ten miles west of Fredericksburg.

On May fifth, Richmond streets were filled with people, shouting and throwing their newspapers into the air. An official dispatch from General Lee to President Davis had just been published. It read:

Milford, May 3d, 1863

To President Davis:

Yesterday Gen. Jackson penetrated to the rear of the enemy and drove him from all his positions from the Wilderness to within one mile of Chancellorsville.

He was engaged at the same time in front of Longstreet's divisions.

Many prisoners were taken, and the enemy's loss in killed and wounded is large.

This morning the battle was renewed.

He was dislodged from all his positions around Chancellorsville, and driven back toward the Rappahannock, over which he is now retreating.

We have again to thank Almighty God for a great victory.

I regret to state that Gen. Paxon was killed, General Jackson severely, and Generals Heth and A. P. Hill slightly wounded.

R. E. LEE
Gen. Commanding.

Many business houses closed for the day. Soldiers marched through the streets, with bands playing Southern airs. Cheering crowds followed them, the sultry weather damping everything except their spirits. A few days later they were shocked and silenced by the news of General Stonewall Jackson's death. He had died from wounds received in the battle which ended with the victory they had just

148

celebrated. Confederate troops had mistaken him and his staff for the enemy and fired upon them as they returned to their own lines. They carried him to a home some distance from the battlefield, where his wife and child were staying. At the last moment, in delirium, he called for General A. P. Hill to bring his men into the fight, then paused a moment to add, "No, no, let us pass over the river, and rest under the shade of the trees." They were his last words.

Immediately, arrangements were made for ceremonies to be held when his remains arrived in Richmond at noon on May eleventh. At that hour all business was suspended and almost the entire population gathered at the depot. There it was announced that the train had been delayed and would not arrive until four o'clock. Most of the crowd dispersed but returned later to join those who had remained.

The tolling of the different church bells signaled the train's approach and preparations were made by the military for the reception of the General's remains. At Broad and Fourth streets, the train stopped, and the coffin was removed to a hearse surmounted by raven plumes and drawn by two white horses. The coffin was enveloped in the flag of the Confederacy, with a large wreath of evergreen on top of it. Those who were to join in the procession to Capitol Square took their places, the military with reversed arms. The command was given, and the vast throng moved slowly along behind the cortege while a band played a dirge and the church bells continued to toll.

Troops had formed in double lines across Capitol Square, past Washington's monument, and on to the Governor's Mansion. The coffin

Cannon at Chancellorsville where General Stonewall Jackson was accidently shot by his own men. *National Park Service.*

Generals Stonewall Jackson and
Lee. *Valentine Museum.*

General Jackson and staff. (The second initial of Jackson above his picture is incorrect.) *Confederate Museum.*

House at Guinea Station in which Stonewall Jackson died. *De Renne Collection, Confederate Museum.*

was carried down the line and placed in the large reception room of the Mansion. That night the body was embalmed, and on the following morning the coffin was again placed in the hearse to be conveyed through the streets in a roundabout way to the Capitol. It was followed by the President, Vice-President, and prominent officials of the city, state, and national governments. In the Hall of the Senate, surrounded by a myriad of flowers, the General's remains lay in state before continuing the journey to his former home in Lexington, Virginia, where interment was to be made.

Prompted by past events and a realization of present needs, the City Council put into effect a plan for a military organization of its citizens to defend Richmond against any sudden attack from the enemy. The Council believed that there was every reason to expect a repetition of the Yankee raid which had recently occurred near the city and that all able-bodied men should be properly trained to meet such an emergency. They were not subject to any routine military duty, or service beyond the city's defenses, but had to be ready at any given signal to go into action on the home front. "Rumors of Yankee raiders are still numerous, yet no one is disconcerted by them," said the press. "Business progresses as usual, and everyone seems satisfied that our soldiers can take care of such matters."

On the Fourth of July, the "Citizens Soldiers were out in force, and flags fluttered in the breeze; but the first were making no holiday parades, and the last were the glorious banners under which Southern arms have repeatedly vanquished a cruel foe, and under which our gallant heroes are again marching to victory." For two days the news from Gettysburg had brightened the hopes of the South. Lee had driven the Yankees in confusion through the town to Cemetery Ridge, but, before evening, they had re-formed their lines and Lee had been forced to retreat. Reports from Vicksburg were even more disheartening. General J. C. Pemberton had surrendered the city to General Ulysses S. Grant. As usual, train after train arrived in Richmond with the sick and wounded. Some six thousand captured Yankees were also brought in and sent to Libby Prison.

In the crowd of civilians gathered at the Danville depot were three women who acted rather suspiciously. A detective questioned them, and, not being satisfied with their answers, took them to Major Griswold, the Provost Marshal, for further examination. There it was discovered that all three women had bladders attached to their person which were filled with liquor they were attempting to smuggle into the city. How the Provost Marshal's office made the discovery was not reported. "After an admonition suitable to the gravity of the offense," Major Griswold kept the liquor and discharged the women.

William A. Jackson, President Davis's coachman. *Harper's Weekly.*

Gettysburg, a Brady photograph taken immediately after the battle. The town remained in the possession of the Confederates during the battles of July 2 and 3, 1863. *National Park Service.*

That same day several flag-of-truce boats arrived from City Point for an exchange of prisoners. On one boat were a number of civilians who had passports permitting them to travel by that route. Among the passengers was Mrs. Robert S. Todd, stepmother of Mrs. Abraham Lincoln. She was on her way South to visit her daughter, Mrs. B. H. Helm, widow of the Confederate Brigadier General who was killed at Chickamauga. She saw several thousand captured Yankees waiting to board the boats vacated by a like number of Confederate soldiers who had just been released from northern prisons.

William A. Jackson, the President's coachman, was not among them. He had recently walked into the Yankee lines near Richmond and, asked what he was doing there, answered that he was on his way to Washington. He had no trouble reaching the Federal Capital; in fact the Yankees helped him on his way. He was described as about thirty years of age, fairly intelligent; he was proud that he could read and write, and signed his name to prove it. He spoke very well and replied in a friendly manner when interviewed. He said he had a wife and three children—all slaves. His former owner had hired him out as a court messenger and hack driver before Mr. Davis purchased him and his family. The Negroes in Richmond, he said, were not allowed to talk about the war; such news was kept from

General A. P. Hill, who initiated the attack that began the Battle of Gettysburg. *Confederate Museum.*

151

Civilians arrived by flag of truce boats at Rocketts Landing. *Valentine Museum*.

Broadway Landing near City Point where prisoners were exchanged. *National Archives*.

them, but they knew what was going on. They were not trusted with arms, either, although their owners relied upon their fidelity. The slaves had no Confederate money, or very little of it, but no one in Richmond would accept it anyway if he could avoid doing so. The President, according to William, seemed disheartened and complained that the popular support of the war was far from what it should be. It was evident that this feeling had affected Mrs. Davis too, for she had all the books, pictures, and a great deal of clothing packed, and was ready to leave Richmond at a moment's notice. He said he sure was glad to be in the North.

Reports that President Davis was ill greatly alarmed the public. His health was indifferent at best, and he had suffered another severe attack of nervous dyspepsia brought on by the cares and duties of his office. A statement by his physician that he had been able to leave his bedroom and walk about his house was published "to relieve the anxiety entertained for his situation."

The attention of the public was also called to the President's proclamation which appeared in all the Richmond newspapers. It informed persons between the ages of eighteen and forty-five who had not enrolled for military service, or, having enrolled, had failed to appear at the conscript camp, that they would be held as deserters and punished accordingly.

"Now, a deserter, in time of war, is punished by death," noted a reporter, "and that is the penalty which hangs over the head of every man in Richmond who fails to do as the law requires. On other occasions when such calls have been made, there were innumerable requests for exemption under the most frivolous and disgraceful pretexts. The enrolling officers have become sharp by practice, and now they are also under the eyes of the powers that be. Let not any man in this city fancy that he sees the door open to evasion and escape, through the leniency of the judges, or the mercy of the Executive. It is determined to enforce the law with the most unsparing vigor, for courts martial and Executives alike have come to the conclusion that mercy to the deserter is cruelty to the country."

The problems of Richmond residents were as varied as the weather. Dog days were back again and dogs were overrunning the city, snatching food wherever they could find it. Merchants at the open markets declared that the dogs had devoured enough produce from their stalls to fatten a dozen droves of hogs which might have been butchered to feed the army. Parents were afraid to let their children play in the yards or in the streets, realizing the danger of the dogs biting them and the possibility of rabies. "Mr. Mayor, what are you going to do about the dogs?" asked the press.

The Mayor said he was being hounded more than the hounds, but that he would get some nets and send out the police to catch every vile cur running at large in the city. He reminded the citizens that if each one would rid his own property of the pests it would greatly aid the police in relieving the community of the curse placed upon it. With the heat at a degree which turned fat men into grease spots, and parched the lean men to such an extent that their bones rattled like skeletons, the police chased the dogs, and the dogs chased the police.

"The Dog War," was one newspaper's heading in its column of local matters. "The police made an assault upon the dog army around the First Market yesterday morning, and, by a dexterous use of their nets, speedily filled the cages with the prowling curs that infest the streets. If taken to the nitre bed and properly used, they will do something to atone for the many sleepless nights they have given to everyone in this city, including the sick and wounded soldiers at the hospitals." But, like Yankees, the dogs kept on coming back to places from which they had retreated, and it took several weeks to exterminate the yelping mongrels.

The lull in war news was broken in late September by a broadside inserted in one newspaper telling of desperate fighting near Chattanooga, Tennessee. THE CONFEDERATE ARMY VICTORIOUS read boldface type, followed by a telegram from General Braxton Bragg,

General Braxton Bragg, C.S.A. *Cook Collection, Valentine Museum.*

on the twenty-first of that month, announcing, "We hold the entire battlefield, and are pressing the enemy today." The broadside, publishing the welcome news from the commander of the Confederate forces there, had been rushed into print too soon. Engagements at Lookout Mountain, the Battle above the Clouds and the storming of Missionary Ridge by Federal troops under the commands of Generals George H. Thomas and Joseph Hooker had turned the tide of victory in favor of the Yankees. In October, President Davis arrived in Atlanta.

"The President is now with the Army of Tennessee," wrote a war correspondent to the Richmond press. "What is the object of his visit? Has he come to mingle with his soldiers and encourage them with his presence? Or has he come to compose the strifes of officers brought about by Bragg's defeat, and, if need be, institute a change in the command of his army? . . . Should such a change be deemed advisable, the prevailing opinion here is that it will be either General Lee or General Longstreet."

Upon Mr. Davis's return to Richmond, it

was reported that his visit to the South had a cheering effect on the army and the people. Nothing was said of the difficulties between Bragg and his staff officers, and he was still in command. The press hailed Mr. Davis as the man who had the confidence and affection of the country in the guidance of her affairs. "If he has committed errors," declared one editorial, "that is only to say that he is human. Where should we have found the perfect man? If there are others who would have avoided these errors, what guarantee have we that they would not have committed others of a more serious character? . . . Who ever saw the hero of the Scotch cap and cloak in the neighborhood of gunpowder? Always ensconced in Washington, devoting all his faculties to the preservation of his own cowardly carcass from the perils into which he hurls other men, as pusillanimous as he is cruel, Abraham Lincoln has made himself the most contemptible of all the despots of modern times, for not one of them can be mentioned who refused to share the hardships and dangers of his subjects in time of war. Well may the South be proud of its President, who, in every public and private relation, is representative of its own character and men."

Despite the Emancipation Proclamation in the North, the price of slaves in Richmond had increased. At a recent auction a Negro man had sold for $3,350, a Negro cook woman for $3,800, and a young Negro girl for the same price. These were reported as the highest prices ever paid for Negroes in the city. The amount offered for the capture and return of runaways had almost doubled since the first of the year. "There seems to be no doubt now that most of the negroes who have lately run away from their masters in this neighborhood have been furnished with forged passes by parties regularly engaged in that business, and that the Yankees have agents in our midst who spare no efforts to entice off servants," one reporter claimed. "There is but one trouble in the way of capturing these bold operators, and that is the lack of white witnesses to prove the transactions."

Dreaming of emancipation, the Negroes in

Rewards for the capture of runaway slaves increased during the War.

"Sensation among 'Our Colored Brethren' on ascertaining that the Grand Performance to which they had been invited on New Year's Day was unavoidably postponed to the year 1900!" *Harper's Weekly*.

Negroes celebrate the announcement of Emancipation in the North by enjoying the comforts of their master's home during his absence. *Harper's Weekly*.

Richmond were getting out of hand. More slaves were going at large and breaking ordinances in other respects. If the master was away, they took over his home. They rode about in public vehicles and held meetings which were unlawful. The only officials authorized by the city ordinance to license more than five Negroes to meet at any one time were the Mayor, if in the city, or, in his absence, the Recorder. If both were absent, the duty fell to the Senior Alderman. Certain justices had been granting permission to the Negroes to hold religious meetings at which they indulged in a great many more things than praying, and the Mayor was asked to investigate such matters. His Honor confessed that he knew of such proceedings, and having found out that the Negro meetings had become so frequent of late, he had laid down the law to them. He was then informed that the Negroes had told the police that he had given permission for some of the gatherings.

On his part, the Mayor said, he wished the police to understand that, having seen so much evil resulting from the meetings, he would in the future refuse such approval, and if the police should find any Negroes gathered together with consent purporting to come from him, it should be disregarded as evidence of insanity on his part. His Honor referred to the great difficulty experienced by white persons each evening in hiring hacks because most of them were filled with Negroes driving about the streets at a rapid pace, and assured the citizens that he would put an end to all the wide privileges which the Negroes were enjoying in the city.

Turning from local matters, the press chided the Yankees, calling attention to their boast of "crushing Lee" before the first of December and eating their Christmas dinner in Richmond. "It is not exactly plain whether the advance on Richmond is to be made by the James river or the Peninsula, or direct from the Rappahannock," scoffed one reporter. "Either way will suit us if it suits General Meade. We hope his heart will not fail him this time, as it did when Lee chased him into his defenses before Washington. Let him come to make a real campaign; a campaign not against the pigs and poultry, but against the fighting men of Lee's army.... We have not the best material for a bowl of eggnog; our white sugar is running low, and our rum growing scarce. But if they will put up with dead-shot whiskey, rifle-barreled, and warranted to kill, they can find plenty at one dollar and a half per drink Confederate currency."

But the captured Yankees did not want to spend Christmas in Richmond, nor did officials want them to do so—if they could get rid of them. Their prisoners now numbered some ten thousand, and those to be exchanged before the holidays could not possibly be accommodated by the few flag-of-truce boats permitted to operate at that time. "Libby Prison is crowded with Yankee officers awaiting an exchange, and the cry is, 'Still they come!'" reported the press. "Every train brings in a fresh batch of these precious Abolition jewels to be fed and cared for at Government expense. They are as thick as blackberries at harvest time, and winter quarters on Belle Isle have had to be enlarged to make room for twenty thousand, which will be about the total at the rate they are coming into Richmond now. Confederate authorities will never admit that negroes are the equals of white men, and these prisoners can thank Abe Lincoln for being here."

Unknown to many, high officials of the Confederate Government had refused to deal with General Ben Butler, in charge of arranging the exchange of prisoners for the Federal Government. No man was hated more than the "Beast of New Orleans," and Commissioner Ould, in charge of the exchange for the Confederate Government, had been ordered by President Davis to have nothing to do with Butler, and, until someone replaced him, to suspend the usual exchange of prisoners. No agreement was reached between the two governments until the end of December, when flag-of-truce boats resumed the exchange of prisoners at City Point and Richmond—too late for thousands of soldiers in the North and in the South, to reach their homes for the holidays that year.

The high prices of all available articles necessary for a real celebration, and the total absence of some, were responsible for a quiet Christmas day in Richmond. The barrooms were open in the morning, and young men and old ones indulged their appetites for stimulating beverages to a limited extent; but, because of the horrid compounds which they imbibed, drinking parties retired early to nurse headaches and nauseated stomachs, thereby relieving the thoroughfares of their presence. Comparatively few inebriates were seen during the evening, and unless their "insides were copper-fastened," they were not able to rally after dark.

In private circles the day was appropriately observed—many persons dividing what abundance they had with their needy neighbors, thus contributing to their own happiness. If the family trees were not loaded with the usual amount of "Yankee trash, and the juveniles were less bountifully supplied by old Kris Kringle, they were blessed with substantials of home growth, and were consoled with the reflection that their spare change had been better spent in providing for the wants of the gallant soldiers who were battling for their protection and their rights on the battlefields."

Many members of the City Council entertained at the City Hall during the afternoon, having as their guests the Representatives who could not be at their own homes that day since Congress was still in session. There was enough eggnog to go around, and speeches were made by those who felt like rending the air with platitudes. Mayor Mayo was present and did much to help the strangers enjoy being in Richmond. How the Mayor felt the following day may be surmised by this report:

"The Mayor, on Saturday, had a good sized army of white men before him, all charged with violating the rules of decency and the laws of the State by getting drunk on Christmas beverages, and annoying sober people. A party of young men, after imbibing freely, made Broad street hideous with their yells—alarmed the residents by kicking at doors—and crying fire at the top of their voices. After a few potations of the distilled damnation now served to the worshippers of Bacchus, it is not surprising that they forgot all sense of propriety and became turbulent and disorderly. The Mayor held them to bail to keep the peace.

"A soldier, after seeing the elephant, ran his head through a window, breaking the glass and cutting his face in several places. When he came into Court, he was well marked with blood and bruises, the fruits of his charge in the old king's fortifications, which have never been carried by storm. He was sent to the Provost. A white woman, for wearing men's apparel in the streets, and a white man for accompanying her, were held to bail; and two women, for hair-pulling and cat scratching, were put in limbo."

A few days later the press added a footnote to the troubles the Mayor was having: "A leak in the roof of the City Hall is seriously injuring the plastering and floors, and needs prompt attention. Yesterday morning the water was dripping through the ceiling into the Mayor's courtroom, very much to the annoyance of the members of the bar and others having business with His Honor."

There never was a dull day at the City Hall in Richmond. *Virginia Historical Society*.

A reception by the President and Mrs. Davis at the Executive Mansion. *Valentine Museum.*

Nervous Dyspepsia

The President's reception at the Executive Mansion on New Year's Day, 1864, gave the public an opportunity to form an opinion regarding his health. He did not appear too well, and many thought that he should not have attempted the long journey southward so soon after his recent illness. The press noted that "the crowd was large and respectable in character. Each person was welcomed by the President and received by his lady. The reception was devoid of that snobbery which attends the levees of the vulgar tycoon who occupies the Presidential chair in Washington, and was in all respects worthy of the President of a great people struggling against the oppressions of a barbarous vandalic enemy." Mr. Davis was still much concerned over the attitude of the people toward the war. Too many thought it would end "tomorrow," instead of working and fighting today and letting tomorrow take care of itself.

The inauguration of the new Governor, William Smith, and the Lieutenant Governor, Samuel Price, at the Capitol that New Year's Day was also well attended. The ceremonies, in the Hall of the House of Delegates, were plain and simple. The Confederate Congress, accompanied by the former Governor, John Letcher, and others, entered the Hall at noon and were loudly greeted by the patriots. Governor Smith proceeded to the Speaker's chair, and, without introduction, read his inaugural address. The opinions he expressed conformed to those of the President; if the people were to win the war, they must win it today, not tomorrow.

"Governor Smith, Commander-in-Chief of the militia, is a soldier, as well as a statesman," declared the press, "and having every confidence in the power of the South to sustain itself against the Federal hordes, and in the indomitable will of Virginia to win her freedom at the point of the bayonet, will promptly organize the militia for defensive operation, and gladly lead them to the field when their services are needed. True steel himself, he had but to ask the people to follow where he will lead, and they will do it." It was announced that the President, beginning on the eighteenth of the month, would hold receptions at the Executive Mansion every Tuesday evening, and the Governor would do likewise at his residence every Friday evening.

The endless attempts to bolster the hopes of the people began to be less optimistic. The truth was beginning to be filtered with honest doubts, but the press kept hammering away on the assumption that the noise would distract from the facts confronting them. Mr. Davis had been President just long enough to give the Confederacy the ailment he was suffering—nervous dyspepsia. Had he let "Doctor Lee" take care of him earlier, instead of sending him to the mountains, the Confederacy might not have contracted the same malady.

The South had a little more than a Grant in Lee, but a hundred times less in Davis than the North had in Lincoln. Of the Northern leaders, it can be said that Lincoln, crafty and patient, could always wait; Grant, determined and aggressive, made Lincoln's waiting active. Of the Southern leaders, Mr. Davis's mirror was too narrow for him to view anyone but himself; there was no room for Lee in so small a space, and he was too often left alone in the wilderness.

"It is painful to observe," said an editorial, "that a certain degree of despondency, whether derived from the tone of Congress or the Jeremiads of the press, is stealing over our people, especially here in Richmond, and that the Yankees are building the largest expectations upon it. What is there in the present aspect of affairs, other than there has been from the opening of the war, to make us despond? What are we suffering now which we ought not to have anticipated, and which, indeed we did not anticipate. . . . Did we not know from the first, at least did not everybody foresee, except a few gentlemen claiming to be wiser than all the rest of the world, that the war would be long, desperate, and tedious! We have had losses and they are neither small nor few in number.

"We are somewhat straitened for provisions. Who, among us all, ever expected that it would be otherwise in the course of the war? When we entered upon it, we took all its chances. We embraced them all without hesitation, as the only alternative left, unless we chose to submit to the Yankees without a struggle. Should they all descend upon us in their turn, or at once, we were prepared to stand the brunt of their combined assault, for we know that, by holding out to the end we must triumph, and that not to triumph would mean to be ruined root and branch, body and soul. Well, we have held out for three years against the most tremendous power ever exerted by any one nation since the world was made.

"Ignored by the whole world, outnumbered by three to one, we have resisted successfully. And shall we be told now—now that our strength is still unbroken, and the hearts of our soldiers are still as high as ever, when those brave men still stand between us and

the subjugation that certainly awaits us if we falter, shall we now be told that the time has come when we are to fold our arms in despair? Who are they that use such language at such an hour?

"Not the soldiers of Lee, or of Johnson, or Longstreet, or of Beauregard. Not those brave men, who have become so accustomed to danger that they barely think of it when it is present. Who are the croakers of the land? Not the farmers, or the people in the country, for they are in general, and with a few shameful exceptions, hopeful and resolute. Who are they? Not the women, for their spirits are too masculine to give way when the storm rises highest. They are the denizens of the towns, the money makers, the men who fear that farther resistance may be the means of cutting all their profits. They hope that if the Yankees come they will not treat them so badly as some seem to anticipate, that they will not use them quite so harshly as they have used the people of New Orleans and Norfolk. That they will not plunder them entirely of the money they have made out of the miseries of the country. These are the croakers. You can tell them at a hundred yards distance when you meet them on the street.

"Congress has it in its power to put into the field an army fully equal in number to that of the Yankees. Indeed, if the stragglers who are scattered all over the country can be brought back to their colors, we feel assured that we have already a force quite equal to the task of repelling any enterprise that the Yankees may undertake, let its scale be as gigantic as it may. Straggling, we are prone to believe, is the result of lax discipline, and discipline is to be expected only from good officers. Let all those regimental and company officers from whose rank the large bodies of men are straggling, be rendered more strictly responsible in the future. Let the penalty be reduction to the ranks, or some other of proportionate severity. Let Congress busy themselves with the discipline of the army, and stop hunting down the poor devils of clerks, who are shivering and starving on $1,500 a year, Memminger currency, and go calmly to work, not act as if they were frightened out of their lives, and things will assume a brighter aspect."

All plans for entertaining the Confederate soldiers and exchange prisoners expected for the holidays were given up when it was announced that the prisoners would not arrive as scheduled. It was then decided to use the money collected for that purpose in providing a New Year's dinner for all the men in the hospitals. "The pretty ladies of our city serving the sick and wounded, helped them forget the past and cheered them for the future," said a reporter. "They worked most of the day and shamed the very few who did nothing more than attend 'eggnog frolics.'"

At the beginning of the year, city officials cracked down on persons who were giving little or no attention to laws recently enacted. One, against paying for army substitutes, started a stampede by many able-bodied men to escape service by other means. Hundreds of them from the wealthier class wrote to government contractors in Richmond, offering to let their slaves work free of charge if they would get the owners exempted from military duty on the grounds that they were essential to their business operations. Since the contractors had to take an oath that they were essential, such men were not able to slip through the military yoke by that dodge, but they tried another escape route to avoid Yankee bullets. "The contractors," said the press, "were no better; they were just a different breed. Their brand of patriotism was unsurpassed in all the history of the human race.

"Patriotism begins at home, and their devotion to their homes is beyond all precedent. The perishable glories of the battlefield fade into insignificance compared with the calm fire-light of the hearth. They would not give the contents of one oyster shell for all the shells that the army have opened since the beginning of the war. Their patriotism is very much akin to that of an old English preacher for his native island. In his last moments, his faithful servant, John, endeavored to console him by saying: 'Be comforted, my good master, you are going to a better place.' 'Ah, John,' said the departing worthy, 'there is no place like Old England.' There is no place, in the

Substitute notices in the Richmond *Dispatch*.

SUBSTITUTE NOTICES.

WANTED—A SUBSTITUTE for a conscript, to serve during the war. Any good man over the age of 35 years, not a resident of Virginia, or a foreigner, may hear of a good situation by calling at Mr. GEORGE BAGBY'S office, Shockoe Slip, to-day, between the hours of 9 and 11 A. M.   A COUNTRYMAN.
[jy 9—1t*]

WANTED—Two SUBSTITUTES—one for artillery, the other for infantry or cavalry service. Also, to sell, a trained, thoroughbred cavalry HORSE.   Apply to   DR. BROOCKS,
Corner Main and 12th streets, or to
                                    T. T. BROOCKS,
jy 9—3t*   Petersburg, Va.

WANTED—Immediately, a SUBSTITUTE. A man over 35 years old, or under 18, can get a good price by making immediate application to Room No. 50, Monument Hotel, or by addressing "J. W.," through Richmond P. O.   jy 9—1t*

WANTED—A SUBSTITUTE, to go into the 24th North Carolina State troops, for which a liberal price will be paid. Apply to me at Dispatch office this evening at 4 o'clock P. M.
jy 9—1t*   R. R. MOORE.

WANTED—A SUBSTITUTE, to go in a first-rate Georgia company of infantry, under the heroic Jackson. A gentleman whose health is impaired, will give a fair price for a substitute. Apply immediately at ROOM, No. 13, Post-Office Department, third story, between the hours of 10 and 3 o'clock.   jy 9—6t*

WANTED—Two SUBSTITUTES for the war. A good bonus will be given. None need apply except those exempt from Conscript. Apply to-day at   GEORGE I. HERRING'S,
jy 9—1t*   Grocery store, No. 56 Main st.

WANTED—Two SUBSTITUTES, over 35 years of age, for which a liberal price will be paid. Address "A," Dispatch office, stating terms.   jy 9—2t*

SUBSTITUTE WANTED—For the war. A man over the age of 35 can get employment as Substitute, by applying at 134 Main street, boarding-house, third story.   jy 9—1t*

WANTED—A SUBSTITUTE for an infantry company. A good price will be paid for one that suits.   Apply at
                    JOHN McDONALD'S Store,
jy 9—3t*   Corner 25th and Broad sts.

A MEMBER of Company H, 15th Regiment Virginia Volunteers, who is in bad health, wishes to procure a SUBSTITUTE. Apply to
                         GEO. F. SMITH, 5th street,
jy 9—3t*   Between Broad and Marshall.

WANTED—SUBSTITUTE—Over 35 years of age. Apply to R. J. FARLEY, Company C, H. R. Miller's 12d Mississippi regiment, at State Fair Grounds.   jy 9—3t*

WANTED—A SUBSTITUTE for Cavalry service. Call on
              DEANE, HOBSON & JAMES.
jy 9—12t*

ANY person wishing to SUBSTITUTE will call at A. Y. STOKES & CO.'S store, between the hours of 10 and 1 o'clock, TO-DAY, 9th inst.
jy 9—1t*

BEAUTIFUL Solid Colored Berages, Satin Striped do.—all colors, cheap, at No. 41 Main st.

BURNETT'S CELEBRATED TOOTH WASH A supply on hand, at No. 4

"Mr. Charles Augustus Slop who was unable to take the field with his regiment because of urgent business." *Library of Congress.*

estimation of some of our most muscular patriots, like their dear native sod. They intend to stick to Virginia like a brother, or what is better and closer, like a leech; to live by her and die in her.

"In general these devoted patriots are huge feeders and drinkers. Men in the prime and vigor of life, and heavily working on important contracts for the Government, they require a vast amount of animal, vegetable, and alcoholic fuel to keep them in operation. They are necessary, however, to the production of supplies for the army. If, from producers, they were converted into consumers, they would use up General Lee's supplies in two days and reduce the Commissary General to a state of total despair. It is a fortunate thing, therefore, that producers, who consume as much as they produce, are not put into the army, where they would produce nothing, not even themselves on the day of battle. If such a patriot saves his country in any field, it must be the cornfield."

Now that military service was demanded of them, and even their money could not buy substitutes, they were fleeing northward like wolves before the hunter. "STOP THE RUN-AWAYS!" screamed the press, with no reference to the Negroes. "What are our authorities thinking of in granting passports to people enabling them to leave the country, where they have been making fortunes, for the sole purpose of avoiding military duty? What is the use of Congress making laws to fill the army if those for whom the laws are intended are permitted by our own authorities to go, as they are going, in schools every day? We hear of numbers who have done nothing during the war but make money, clearing out now. They urged others to fight, but when they were called upon, they ran in the opposite direction. Some headed for the Chickahommy expecting to reach Yankeeland by that route, but were turned back to face the music. If not closely watched they may yet make a successful flight. Shut down the passport gate at once, or Congress may as well adjourn, so far as filling the army is concerned!"

Some of these able-bodied men who were fleeing from the South and military duty left their families to follow them when they could. Too often, the families obtained employment by saying that their husbands were in the Southern army, thereby taking from loyal citizens the work they needed in order to pay for necessities.

An attempt to stop gambling in the city prompted the enactment of another law which sentenced persons found guilty of operating, or taking part in such operations, to thirty-nine lashes from the whip, a fine, and imprisonment. This did not stop the gambling, and a score of police, with two lieutenants of the night watch, descending on one establishment, seized a Faro table, one silver dealing box, a large number of checks, some packs of playing cards, and about four hundred dollars. They also arrested two white men and four Negroes. At the time the officers entered, no Faro was being dealt, but the trappings were all in readiness for the customers when they arrived.

The Faro dealers knew how to prevent visitors from becoming involved with the law. Every man who entered the room before the "tiger" was regularly uncaged was required to take a seat behind the table, open a small bank, and go through one deal, the others betting against him. After a deal had passed around, so that all had made themselves

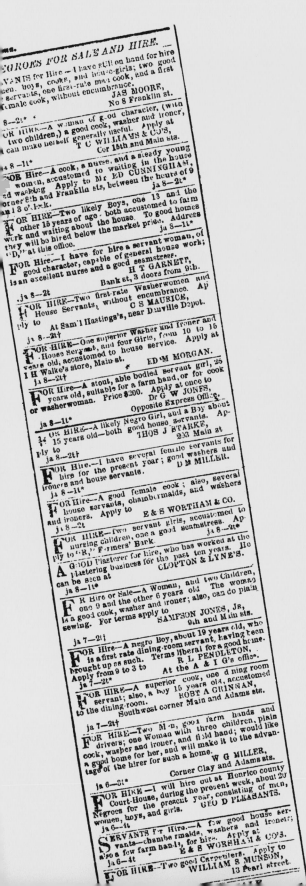

Long list of Negroes for sale and hire regularly appeared in the Richmond *Dispatch*.

"equally amenable to stripes and imprisonment," the real Bengal Tiger took to his lair, and woe to all who approached him. Armed with a double-box loaded with strippers, and without "cue paper" to make the game, the betters found their piles of treasury notes melting away as frost before the sun.

"If the present law does not put an end to faro, then no law can," said the press, "and the best plan would be to license gambling houses, make them public places, and thus keep young men from flocking to the hideouts and squandering their means. The present law, if it can be enforced, is sufficiently severe in the punishment prescribed; but the difficulty of its enforcement is very great."

Before the Mayor could finish his inquiries and get witnesses he needed to convict those arrested, another justice granted the parties bail in the sum of $1,000 each. They failed to appear when called. The new law proved no better than the old, and gambling continued to be a major industry in Richmond.

In an effort to control the exorbitant charges being demanded for the service of Negroes, the government fixed the price at $300 and its agents began impressing them. Authorities contended that was enough to satisfy the slaveholder, when the cost of board and clothing was considered, and no citizen should pay more.

"If the contracts entered into were merely for a day or a month," said the press, "there might be a reason for some increase of hire; but when everyone knows that a radical change is to be made in the currency as speedily as Congress can do it, and that $300 twelve months hence might be worth more than $1,500 now, those who hire out negroes have no right to demand more than the Government price. The Government must have labor, and its agents are right in securing it at once, but in all the country around Richmond, the price is vastly lower than in this city, and it would come down here if people would hold off hiring negroes for a short time." But the black market in hiring blacks soared even higher as the government demand for their services increased from day to day.

163

This traffic brought on an attempt to kidnap slaves going at large in the city. A white man named Elliott was arrested and taken before the Mayor for having in his possession three young slaves. Elliott said the Negroes told him they were born free and he was taking care of them for the night; the Negroes said they were slaves and were being held against their wishes. The Negroes were taken into custody and advertised for their owners to pick up. Elliott was turned over to the Hustings court for trial. There was no one to testify against him and he was discharged. Reports of his other attempts to kidnap slaves turned up in the newspapers from time to time.

The only persons who suffered from the roundup of law breakers at the first of the year were seventeen Negroes who were found in a kitchen on Shockoe Hill. They were brought before the Mayor and sentenced to the lash. The press reminded others of their race that "all the negroes in Richmond know that any assemblage of more than five of them, except at church, is unlawful, and if they will persist in their gatherings, they must expect to be punished."

The post office employees and workers in other government departments were striking, or threatening to strike, for payments due them or an advance in salary to meet the high cost of their everyday needs. Congress gave little heed to their problems and the press defended the employees with two-column blasts against the lack of interest in its citizen patriots.

"Among the most exciting amusements, not beneath the dignity even of members of Congress, (who are known to be the most dignified, intelligent, and exemplary of the human species) is the chase of that description of bipeds known as Government clerks. The game combines all the qualities that are requisite to arouse the energies of true sportsmanship. Its destruction affords pasturage for the hunter's friends, and it has absolutely no powers of resistance. Under the old United States Government the hue and cry against the clerks was as fierce and universal as the Yankee nation, but under that regime they had the advantage of being defended by the party which put them in power, and which made their cause its own. This drawback upon the zest of clerk-hunting does not exist in the Confederate States. They were put in their places without reference to party, and indeed, there are no parties yet in the Confederacy except the pursuers and the pursued.

"Without friends, and helpless as partridges and snowbirds, they present the most tempting target that ever drew a cockney's fire. Nothing so strikingly illustrates the passion of man for sport as the eagerness to pursue animals whose flesh is not good for food and whose plumage is not attractive to the eye. The Government clerks have in general but little meat on their bones, and their raiment is by no means purple and fine linen. The fifteen hundred of Mr. Memminger's assignats which they annually receive scarcely furnished them even with the most meager diet, while their clothing is but the faded and tat-

The Virginia Armory, garrisoned by a company of infantry known as the State Guard. *Valentine Museum.*

The Confederate hero, General John H. Morgan. *Cook Collection, Valentine Museum.*

tered remnants of other days. Not a few of them are old men, refugees from homes once the abodes of comfort and hospitality; others are disabled soldiers, and many having wives and children, whose sufferings from hunger and cold must add the keenest relish to the excitement of the hunt. Some are scholars, men of learning, of eloquence, and of other intellectual gifts, which might add lustre even to the splendor of Congressional intellects.

"We do not mean to intimate that many of them could ever have been elected members of Congress. With the exception of that small minority of their number which exempts itself from performing military duty, imbibes strychnine whiskey, and dallies with the tiger in his jungle, there is not one of them qualified for a national legislator. But scholars, authors, and men of genius, are not wanting among them, and it is pleasant to see such pulled down and degraded, their keen sensibilities lacerated, and the fangs of poverty and the world's scorn fixed in their vitals, and a whole angry pack of hounds and huntsmen helping and yelling for their blood.

"Therefore, hunt them down ye merry Nimrods, with hound and horn! Let there be a generous rivalry which of you will be first at the death. Because there are unworthy per-

sons among them, because there are some skulks, and loafers and drones among them, exceptions unknown in Congressional bodies, give no quarter to any of them. Rob them of a decent support, starve and freeze their wives and children, and plunder them of their good names. They are only clerks and cannot resist. The little plank they hang to, swaying with every wind and tossed with every wave, is the only plank between them and the deep ocean.

"They cannot leave it to fight you. Pelt them with stones, and pour furious broadsides into them from your Congressional three-deckers. And when they sink at last, retire to your honest couches and thank God that you are so magnanimous, and merciful and just."

The arrival of General John H. Morgan in January was a great occasion. He had been expected for several days and the plans made for his reception were all that a hero who had escaped from a Federal prison in Ohio could expect. During his progress through Yankee territory, with an ox whip in his hand, he had passed himself off as a government agent, engaged in buying mules. Barely escaping capture again at various points along the way, he finally reached the Confederate lines at Dalton, Tennessee.

At the Danville depot in Richmond, he was greeted by members of the City Council and a military detachment who escorted him to the Ballard House where a suite of rooms had been prepared for him. After a day's rest, he rode in an open barouche to the City Hall with Mayor Mayo and two councilmen, preceded by the Armory Band and the City Battalion. Other members of the City Council, the Kentucky delegation, and many distinguished military officers followed them in carriages. As the procession passed along Main Street, large crowds lined the sidewalks to get a glimpse of the Confederate hero.

It had been announced in the morning papers that at noon General Morgan would be presented to the citizens of Richmond from the south porch of the City Hall. Notwithstanding the inclemency of the weather, a vast number of civilians, military officers, and soldiers gathered there long before he was due

The Ballard House where General Morgan stayed while in Richmond. *Virginia Historical Society.*

to appear. Many ladies filled the Hustings courtroom in the building where the General was to receive his friends and admirers after his introduction to the public.

At half-past twelve o'clock, the music of the Armory Band signaled the approach of the procession. Loud and prolonged cheers greeted him as he arrived and stepped from his carriage at the entrance to the City Hall where Generals A. P. Hill, Edward Johnson, J. E. B. Stuart, and many other friends awaited him. He was described as being six feet tall, with keen, dark eyes, and features indicative of benevolence, thought, and great courage. His dark hair was stylishly cut, and he wore a moustache and goatee. He was dressed in a citizen suit of black and a military cap.

Short speeches by the Mayor and other officials were answered briefly by the popular General Morgan. He then returned to his carriage for the drive down Governor Street, where cheering crowds greeted him. At the Ballard House he found more distinguished citizens and told them of his plans to reorganize his forces and return to the battle front. Before the end of the year, he was shot down by unknown persons in the house of a friend he was visiting. His remains were brought back to Richmond and given a temporary burial until they could be removed to his native state of Kentucky.

At this time, Jim Dennison, otherwise known as "Pemberton," a slave owned by President Davis, was being greeted in Washington, D.C. Before escaping north, he had served Mr. Davis for nearly twenty years and was well acquainted with all the old residents of the Southern Capital. In Washington he was interviewed by General H. W. Halleck and Secretary of War Edwin Stanton, but they learned no more from him than the trivial incidents of his life in the Davis household.

The Richmond police had been informed that Cornelius, another slave belonging to President Davis, had run away. They succeeded in finding him a few hours after his escape, and lodged him in the upper station house. When caught, he had in his possession enough cold chicken, ham, preserves, and bread to last for a long journey, and a large sum of money stolen from his master. Some time after being locked up he called to the keeper of the prison to give him some water, and, as that gentleman incautiously opened the door of his cell, Cornelius knocked him down and again made his escape. Peter Everett, the only watchman present, started after him, but before running many steps he stumbled and fell, injuring himself severely.

Breaking out of jail was the biggest indoor-outdoor sport in Richmond. Now the city had what the press described as "the most important escape of Yankees from Libby Prison during the war." Of the eleven hundred officers confined there, one hundred nine failed to answer the roll call one morning. Colonel A. D. Streight of the U. S. Fifty-first Indiana regiment had been the prize "guest." He was listed as "a most notorious character," captured in Tennessee by General N. B. Forrest, and charged with having recruited a Negro regiment.

When the Confederate officers in charge of the prison discovered that the Yankees had escaped, they became very excited and used every means to ascertain how it had happened. One of them, a Major Turner, was inclined to believe that the sentinels on duty had been bribed, and this impression was strengthened by several Yankees who remained behind and said that heavy fees had been paid a Confederate officer to influence the guards in their behalf. On learning this, the order was given to place the guards under arrest and commit them to Castle Thunder. Not feeling satisfied about the matter, the Major and a Lieutenant Latouche determined to leave no stone unturned to ferret out the mystery, and proceeded to search every part of the building for further information.

After a fruitless examination, they were about to end their search when the idea struck them that some clue might be obtained by examining the buildings on the opposite side of the street. There they discovered a large hole in the stall of a shed used as a stable, on a line with the street running between it and Libby Prison. The officers were satisfied that they had found the outlet of the escape passage; their next step was to locate the spot where the men had started digging their way to freedom. Some few yards from the eastern end of the basement in the building, they came upon a large piece of granite. This had been removed from the foundation and a tunnel, extending fifty-nine feet across the street eastward, had been cut through to the outlet. The tunnel was about seven feet from the surface of the street, and from two and one-half to three feet square.

The dirt which had accumulated as the work progressed was spread about the back part of the basement and then covered over with a large quantity of straw which had been left there. No one knew how long the prisoners had been engaged in this stupendous undertaking, but with the limited facilities they possessed it was certain that months had elapsed since the work was first begun. The escape had been skillfully managed by master minds and accomplished through the indomitable perseverance of the Yankees. The Confederate officers concluded that further escape through this passage had been contemplated by other prisoners, and their earnestness in trying to throw the blame upon the guards was to prevent inquiry so the tunnel would be left open for their exit to freedom. Had the officers not discovered the tunnel at that time, one more night might have emptied the prison of the whole number confined there. Workmen were brought in to seal up the passage and prevent any more Yankees from departing without the knowledge and consent of the officers in charge. Immediately after the escape was discovered, a Colonel Brown, commanding a cavalry battalion for local defense, was ordered to scour the surrounding country in pursuit of them. Selecting twenty-five men from each company, he started out to find the prisoners. Four of them who had succeeded in escaping were recaptured and brought back late that afternoon. They had gotten about twenty-two miles from the city before they were overtaken.

Scene in Richmond. "The President stands in a corner *telling his beads,* and proclaims a THIRD FAST . . . while . . . the sufferings endured by the people have never been paralleled in history." Quoted from "a Rebel paper" by *Harper's Weekly.*

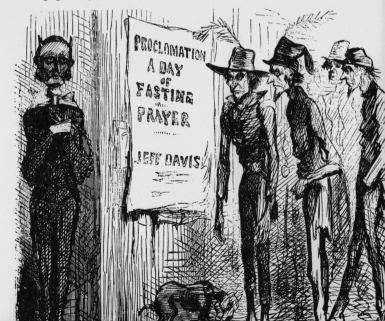

While the search was going on, the officers in charge of Libby Prison were told that some of the Yankees were concealed in the upper rooms of a building occupied by Mahoney & McGehee, on Main Street. Military guards were rushed there and cautiously entered the building. Suddenly there was a scramble by a group of men to reach the roof of the house. Fortunately, the guards did not shoot, for they were all Richmond citizens, not a Yankee among them. The guards had disturbed a gambling establishment and corralled several

Judson Kilpatrick, later commissioned a general. *National Archives.*

congressmen among its patrons on the roof. The raid had caused quite a crowd to collect in the street below expecting to see the notorious Colonel Streight brought down with the other Yankees. He and the majority of the prisoners were never recaptured.

In a city such as Richmond, with evil on all sides and temptations multiplied a thousandfold, one reporter confessed that the observance of Lent was no hardship. In what way it was to be kept that year to distinguish it from other days of fasting and prayer puzzled him. Under the dietetic laws of the Carthusian monks, the brethren were not to eat meat at any time, and during Lent they were prohibited the use of eggs, milk, butter, and cheese. Dry bread and water were their Lenten fare, but as everyone in Richmond knew, dry bread and water had been the daily food of some salaried officials in the city all the year round. "This is not the result of any scarcity of the fruits of the earth, but of the disordered currency," contended the reporter, "for there is no article of food or clothing which cannot be purchased at pretty much the old prices for gold. But whatever the cause, the 'dry eatings' are an established institution, and Lent, instead of forty, lasts three hundred and sixty-five days each year."

In the midst of their preparation for Easter, the people were startled by a report that a secret organization, plotting to assassinate the President and overthrow the government, had been discovered in Richmond. Two foreigners had been arrested and charged with being the leaders of the organization and the chief instigators in the plot. They were committed to Castle Thunder prison, and the public was told that within a few days there would be developments which would lead to the arrests of a hundred or more citizens who were "members of the incendiary association."

The two men were brought before General Winder, but for some reason he concluded that it was not in his power to dispose of the matter and turned them over to the Mayor. When they were taken to his courtroom, a large crowd of curious spectators were on hand to hear how such a fiendish plot could have been concocted under the very eyes of the city's officials. Shortly after the opening of the case, the spectators discovered that a mountain had been made of a molehill and before the Mayor had concluded his investigation, the courtroom was almost empty. It was probable that Mr. Davis himself, during his administration, never knew of several quiet "feelers" among a few high officials to overthrow him and form, in their opinion, a more stable government.

Relief from the exposure of the plot by the "bogus organization" had hardly subsided before the people were given more excitement. Press reports told of the damage done by Yankee troops on the Virginia Central Railroad near Richmond: DARING RAID OF THE ENEMY: THEY APPROACH WITHIN THREE MILES OF THE CITY: THEIR PLANS UNVEILED, read the headlines. "The reader will be startled this morning by the diabolical plans of the Yankee raiders who have just been driven in disappointment and disgrace from the very gates of Richmond," said a report. "A lucky shot has sent to his long account one [Colonel Ulric Dahlgren] of the three leaders under [Judson] Kilpatrick's command and upon his carcass were found the papers which disclosed their whole plan. It was quite complete in itself. Once in the city, the men were 'to keep together and well in hand.' The first achievement cut out for them was to release all the Federal prisoners. Next was the massacre of the President and his entire Cabinet, and the destruction of Richmond—'the hated city'—as one of the orders styles it.

"Besides these events, it was especially enjoined that 'all mills must be burned,' and 'also everything which can be used by the rebels must be destroyed.' Of course, that means everything that is to be eaten or worn! It will be seen that it was further ordered that all 'horses and cattle we (they) do not need immediately must be shot rather than left.' The 'address' setting forth these objects, and signed by Colonel Dahlgren, appeals to the men to engage heartily in the enterprise, and taunts contemptuously any who will decline. To such a man, he says: 'Let him step out, and he may go hence to the arms of his sweetheart and read of the braves who have swept through the city of Richmond!' A memorandum discovered imparts the information that

Colonel Ulric Dahlgren. *National Archives.*

none declined to accompany the gallant and chivalrous Colonel. Not the blandishments of a sweetheart could tempt any of the band of robbers and thieves, to forego the booty and butchery, the robbing and marauding, which would inevitably fall to the lot of the brave. And the pious Dahlgren concludes his address to his cutthroat followers thus: 'Ask the blessing of the Almighty, and do not fear the enemy.'

"The whole plot seemed to have gone awry as it deserved. There were to have been three bands. One to have entered the city on the North, the other two to have approached it by the river, one on the north bank and one on the south. But a delay brought about through the intentional misleading of them by a negro guide, caused the column that was to have crossed the river not to do so. The guide was certainly hung for his services. We are greatly disappointed that Kilpatrick and his hen-roost warriors were not all taken. They tore up a few miles of railroad, which will be replaced in two or three days; burnt a dwelling house, two barns, and a mill, all of which could have been done in one night by a negro not having the fear of the gallows before his eyes; stole a quantity of silver plate from Mr. Morson; set all the hens and turkeys (which seem to have known by instinct that Hen-roost Kilpatrick was coming) to cackling; fled upon the first scent of gunpowder, as though they had been anointed in childhood with brimstone for the itch, and still remembered the horrors of the infliction; and made their way to beast Butler, leaving behind them 200 killed and wounded, 450 prisoners, 700 horses, any quantity of saddles, blankets, and overcoats, and small arms out of numbers. We would add that they left their honor behind them too, but that would not be correct for they had none to leave."

His corpse was brought to the city in a plain white pine coffin. It arrived on the York River railroad train, and remained in the baggage car overnight. A clean, coarse, white cotton shirt and dark blue pants covered the body partially enveloped in a dark military blanket. Colonel Dahlgren was about thirty years old, five feet ten inches in height, and had a long cadaverous face, light hair, slight beard, and

a small goatee. His features were well preserved, but the expression of his face indicated that he had died in pain. Before being transferred to a secret burial place, his body was identified by Captain Dement and a Mr. Mountcastle of Richmond. They had been captured by Dahlgren's raiders and forced to accompany them until he was killed.

The plan to free thousands of Yankee prisoners frightened the military authorities and for several days the bulk of them were sent elsewhere. The raid also alarmed visitors to the city and only a few trains arrived during that week. "Like the hotels of this city, the 'guests' at the Libby have greatly fallen off," noted a reporter. "Only four Yankees had their names booked there yesterday."

When the exchange of prisoners was resumed in larger numbers, it seemed to indicate that the Confederate Government had accepted "Beast Butler" as the representative of the Federal Government in such matters, but that turned out to be untrue. The men sent to be exchanged were paroled prisoners under the cartel before the Confederates had refused to deal with Butler.

On one of the flag-of-truce boats arriving in Richmond, General Custus Lee was among the prisoners. He had been held as hostage by the Federal Government for the safety of Captains Sawyer and Flynn, condemned to be hanged by the Confederate Government in retaliation for two officers executed by General Burnside for recruiting within Federal

"God Save the South," a song which as the war progressed came to have more and more meaning for the people of the Confederacy. *Library of Congress.*

Agnes Lee

Custis Lee

Mary Lee

Mildred Lee

General Lee

Mrs. Lee

W. H. F. Lee

Mrs. R. E. Lee II

Robert E. Lee II

GENERAL LEE AND FAMILY

lines. The captains were returned on the boat which had brought in the paroled Confederate prisoners.

As they docked at the Richmond wharf they were given a great ovation. A procession was formed, and, led by Smith's Band, the crowd marched to Capitol Square, where they were greeted by President Davis and Governor Smith, both of whom addressed the arrivals enthusiastically. General Robert E. Lee came to Richmond to see his son but no publicity was given the visit. A friend who traveled with him from Gordonsville to the Capital said he was very hale and vigorous, and looked as though there were still a dozen

Residence of General Lee and his family in Richmond, now the Virginia Historical Society. *Virginia Historical Society.*

or more good campaigns in him. He was affable, polite, and unassuming, and shared the discomforts of a crowded railroad coach with ordinary travelers.

The General had no staff or other attendant with him, and talked freely about affairs other than the army and the country. At one station where an eager crowd was gazing at him, he suddenly remarked, "I suppose these people are speculating as to what is on foot now." He spoke quickly, sometimes brusquely, and with the tone of one accustomed to command. The General was as unostentatious and unassuming in dress as he was in manner. He wore a Colonel's coat (three stars without the wreath), badly faded, blue pantaloons, high-top boots, and a high felt hat without ornament save a small cord around the crown. At this time Lee was offered a home in the Capital as a gift from the people of Richmond. His letter to the President of the City Council said:

"Sir: My attention has been directed to a resolution reported in the newspapers as having been introduced into the body over which you preside, having for its object the purchase by the city of Richmond of a house for the use of my family.

"I assure you, sir, that no want of appreciation of the honor conferred upon me by this resolution, or insensibility to the kind feeling which prompted it, induces me to ask, as I most respectfully do, that no further proceedings be taken in reference to the subject. The house is not necessary for the use of my family, and my own duties will prevent my residence in Richmond. I should, therefore, be compelled to decline the generous offer, and trust that whatever means the City Council may have to spare for this purpose may be devoted to the relief of the families of our soldiers in the field, who are more in want of assistance and more deserving of it than myself."

The City Council acknowledged his letter and said that they hoped he might be persuaded to accept the offer at a later date. Before the end of the year, however, Lee rented a home in Richmond where his family was living when he returned there after the war.

General Lee at the close of the War. *Virginia Historical Society.*

Strangely enough the newspaper in which Lee's letter appeared also published this not too flattering description of the Capital, which might have cautioned others not to live there. According to the Charleston *Courier*: "Richmond has been destroyed, and a new city built on and over its ruins. The Richmond of old, the site of residences of gentlemen, of elegant hospitalities and social virtues, with the combined advantages of city and country life and culture, is no more, but in its place has been erected a new Richmond, after the moral model of Sodom and New York and Washington. Great and good old Virginia, mother of States and statesmen, has done and suffered much for the Confederacy, and has suffered much from the Yankees, but the severest blow she has yet received is the invasion and occupation of the Confederate Congress; and the transformation of her Richmond into a Confederate metropolis. Alabama, Georgia, or any other state would and could have endured this subjugation with less injury, since they are farther from the border and the sight of Washington. We are acquainted with places like the Federal Capital where rascality, licentiousness, villainy, and corruption abound, and which now have been so faithfully transferred to the Confederate Capital, and we are amazed that a city of professedly Christian people, who are supposed to elect, and be represented by their best men, will tolerate such evil."

If the reputation Richmond had acquired among her sister cities influenced the Confederate Government in removing the lady clerks of the Treasury Note Bureau to Columbia, South Carolina, no rumor to that effect was reported. The note-signers received notice that they were to travel by a special train leaving "preciously" at five o'clock on the day of their departure. They were warned to be prompt, that each could take but one trunk on the train, and that other baggage and effects must be deposited at the Treasury office to go by freight with the furniture. The press condemned the whole procedure on the grounds that their removal was of no benefit either to the government or to those employed, since the notes, after being signed, had to be sent back to Richmond before they could be circulated. The removal also would interrupt the issuing of the new for the old currency, the press contended, at a time when public sentiment and action were aiding the government in taking care of its finances. That this removal might relieve Richmond of a few hundred mouths to be fed was of no benefit to the city. Many of them had families who had lost everything and taken refuge in Richmond, and to send them away would deprive aged fathers and mothers, and young brothers and sisters of all that kept the wolf of starvation from their door. "We say nothing about the honor of Virginia, which is involved in the avoidance of everything that looks like the removal of the seat of government from its beleaguered Capital," argued the press. "Virginia, on a former occasion, when far more closely environed by the hosts of the enemy than she is ever likely to be again, uttered a memorable voice, 'she treads no steps backwards.' When peace returns to bless the land then let the Capital be removed, if necessary; but not now—not while danger threatens— not till Virginia, which has borne and suffered so much, shall vindicate her right and might, and in company with her Confederate allies, plant her foot on the neck of the prostrate tyrant."

Below the editorial protesting the removal of the lady clerks was this special notice: "In consequence of the deranged state of the currency, our auction sale advertised for tomorrow will be postponed for one week. Tardy & Williams."

Harassed by the fear of an impending attack on the city, the President suffered the loss of his five-year-old son, Joseph. The boy had been playing in the yard during the early part of the evening when a servant went to look for him and returned saying that he was missing. A search was made, and the boy was found lying insensible on the brick terrace below the east portico of the Mansion. His left thigh was broken and he had a severe concussion on his forehead. A stepladder, leading from the terrace to the porch about twenty feet above, was evidence that the boy had been on the ladder and, losing his balance, had fallen to the bricks below. The President's eldest son, Jefferson, tried to make his brother speak, but he did not respond. Doctors were called in, but all their efforts to revive the boy were ineffective, and an hour later he died. Funeral services held at St. Paul's Episcopal Church were attended by many sympathetic friends of the family.

A new string of headlines now haunted the people of Richmond: THE IMPENDING BATTLE ON THE RAPIDAN: THE ENEMY ON THE PENINSULA: IRONCLADS AND TRANSPORTS IN THE JAMES RIVER: THE GRAND MOVEMENT ON RICHMOND. "The last grand combined movement of the Yankees with their auxiliary hordes of foreigners and negroes to get possession of this city is still pending," said the press, "with (to use a favorite phrase of theirs) its 'back broken.' In all the collisions between Grant's immense column and the invincible army under General Lee, the advantage has been decidedly in our favor. While we have every reason to believe that Grant's army, driven from field to field by our intrepid troops, must be to a great extent demoralized, yet a complete defeat is wanting to wind him up and send him to the Hades of all defeated Yankee Generals. On the James river the enemy seems inclined to press the amphibious part of the combined attack against Richmond, Grant or no Grant. It is said that Butler commands; and he has vanity and ambition enough to delude him into the idea that he may, after all, be the lucky man to take Richmond, and thus become the most renowned individual in all the Yankee nation! He is not so much of a vulture as Seward, nor equal as an ass to Lincoln. He is more of a buzzard than an eagle, but he is not the only buzzard in the Yankee camps.

"The great battle between the armies of Lee and Grant in Spotsylvania, appears to have been one of the most sanguinary and hotly contested of the war. General Lee holds the position he took in when, marching by the right flank of the enemy who had abandoned

Generals Stonewall Jackson, J. E. Johnston, and Robert E. Lee. *National Park Service.*

his entrenchments on the Germanna road, he forced him to incline toward Fredericksburg, and has kept him at bay for a week, inflicting upon him heavy losses every time he has sought to turn his flank. The situation on the Rappahannock is encouraging. When Grant proclaims that he will not recross the river as long as he has a man, he employs the language of a braggart, which rather shows the madness of desperation than brave determination. He has proved, however, that he will fight, if not wisely, certainly earnestly."

Lee, too, knew that Grant would fight as predicted, and that the final siege in the long and bloody War between the States was closing in upon him. The people in Richmond, as Yankee guns continued to roar over Petersburg, began to check their own timetable with that of Grant. There was some delay all around; no one seemed to be exactly on time. But on May eleventh, time did not matter. Everything in Richmond stopped but the ticking of the clocks. The city was silent, the people were silent. Every man was on the home-front battleline. The day passed; the night passed. Then, on the following afternoon came word that the Yankees had been beaten back once again—and once again the people of Richmond relaxed.

On the day of the expected attack, all local forces, including reporters and printers, were on military duty and publications were suspended. Now they were back at work turning out the news. Several other Richmond employees, temporarily unoccupied while awaiting events, got restless and began looking for trouble. According to one reporter, they did not have far to go. "Three of the clerks of the Central Railroad Company being at leisure, owing to the stoppage of business on their road, thought to amuse themselves by walking out and taking a shot at the enemy north of the city. Carefully loading their guns, they strolled out the Central road to our entrenchments. Here they found all quiet, and our men in the earthworks told them there was no danger in proceeding further, as our pickets were still some distance ahead of them. Assured by this information, they continued

General Grant's lines in the vicinity of Richmond. *National Archives.*

"Military gymnastics, or the greased pole in Virginia—
why the Union generals don't take Richmond." *Frank
Leslie's Illustrated Newspaper.*

their walk across a wheat field in front of our
line and in the direction of a heavy piece of
woods on the left of the railroad. On getting
within three hundred yards of this wood,
they perceived a line of troops drawn up in
battle array, and the line looking particularly
blue, they began to suspect they were ventur-
ing upon dangerous ground, and halted to
confer and reconnoiter. But any doubts they
may have had as to who were before them
were readily solved by a volley of a hundred
muskets. The hostile bullets whistled about
their ears most uncomfortably. The hunters
threw themselves on the ground without loss
of time, and one of them dived into the soft
mud up to his ears. Afraid to rise or look back
in this woeful predicament, they bethought
themselves of trying the efficiency of a flag of
truce, and simultaneously pulled out their

white pocket handkerchiefs and waved them
in a frenzied manner. This however was far
from having the desired effect, for the Yankees instantly opened on them again, and har-
rowed up the mud about them in a style
which taught them the necessity of changing
their base.

"Failing in their flags of truce, they sprang
to their feet and ran for their lives. At every
step the Yankee bullets hurried them. They
had a quarter of a mile to run, and made it
in the shortest time on record. Luckily none
of them was hit, and breathless and spattered
with mud to the crowns of their heads, they
at last ran safely into our lines, where they
were received with such yells and cheers as
have seldom waked the echoes of the Chickahominy. All three of the gentlemen express
themselves as thoroughly satisfied for the
present on the subject of Yankee hunting, and
say the next time they go out it will be in
rather stronger force."

By the middle of May, the Yankees had not
yet taken Richmond. The large force under
Butler had been "performing a dance of forward and backward and crossovers" on the
James River without acquiring any advantage
since the day it landed. The opinion was that
if Lee finally defeated Grant, the Yankees'
General would have to go home and would
not be allowed to run for the Presidency. It
was conceded, however, that Grant was likely
to persevere to the end.

"Our people have become so accustomed
to these marches upon Richmond, and the
lesser raids of the enemy, that they are no
longer excited by them," acknowledged the
press. "The citizen leaves his home, his office,
or his shop, in a quiet and orderly manner, as
if he were going on a matter of private and
not at all exciting business; and the women
of Richmond look upon the departing columns
of citizen soldiers—their fathers, husbands,
brothers, friends—not only resignedly, but
cheerfully, proud indeed of the gallantry of
those upon whom they lean, in repairing to
the point of danger to defend their city."

In the Confederate forces was the thirty-
one-year-old General J. E. B. Stuart. He had
been harassing the Yankees with cavalry
raids and had captured some mules from them.

General J. E. B. (Jeb) Stuart. *Valentine Museum.*

General Stuart and his cavalry on a scouting expedition. *Illustrated London News.*

He didn't like their looks, and sent a telegram to Quartermaster General Montgomery Meigs at Washington requesting him, in the future, to furnish his own troops with a better breed since the mules he had captured were very inferior.

During a raid near the Globe Tavern, a few miles from Richmond, "Jeb" was wounded and died the following day. On May fourteenth, it was announced that his body had been brought to the city for burial. The funeral services, at St. John's Episcopal Church, were conducted by the Rev. Joshua Peterkin. The President, high-ranking military and government officials, members of Congress, and many distinguished citizens attended and followed his remains to Hollywood Cemetery where he was buried.

On the battlefront, Grant had sent Lee a flag of truce requesting an interval in the fighting so unarmed parties could care for the wounded and bury the dead. The removal of decaying carcasses was a relief to the soldiers, whose position was becoming almost intolerable from the stench.

The Yankees now began to pound away at nearby Petersburg. Under General A. V. Kautz they made several assaults upon defenses southwest of the city, but were driven back each time. At Harrison's Landing the Yankee cavalry advanced on the Salem Church road and Malvern Hill, and were driven back again by General Fitzhugh Lee. The Yankees kept blasting the Confederate lines, but did not get through. With stores closed and her men on the battlefront, the place looked like a deserted village. It was evident in Richmond that the Yankees considered Petersburg the gateway to their city.

That Fourth of July, the Richmond press noted: "On the last anniversary Grant occupied Vicksburg. Today he was to be in Richmond. Now he says, 'I shall adhere to this line if it takes all summer.' This must be a typographical error. Insert 'lying' instead of 'line' and then his boast makes sense and truth. It is more than two months since he crossed the Rapidan. He is still in his place, Butler is in his place, and Richmond is in its place. With the capture of Richmond, the war is to end, the principal rebels are to be executed, the plantations and negroes of the South are to pass to Northern proprietors, its mighty States are to dwindle into subjugated territories, and the Republic move on with a momentum and majesty which will astonish and overawe the world. The American eagle, with one wing overshadowing the Atlantic and the other the Pacific, and with the Southern Confederacy struggling helplessly in his talons, will soar aloft and scream, 'Oh, puissant and irresistible Ulysses! Oh, memorable and immortal Fourth of July, 1864!'" The press also reported that at every point on the enemy's lines huge flags of the United States were being displayed, and their bands were incessantly playing unfamiliar tunes.

Since the appearance of Grant's army in the vicinity of Richmond, untold misery had been inflicted upon those citizens who were residing in the neighborhood occupied by them. Some were caught between the two armies, and, as a natural consequence, their houses and other property had been destroyed and the occupants themselves compelled to beat a hasty retreat. Many had been forced to leave

mies, both the blue and the gray. Eventually some returned to what had been their homes only to find the bare land dotted with a few skeletons and skulls of men who had been there during their absence.

One balmy summer day, Miss Doctor Mary Walker, the Yankee "surgeoness" captured in Tennessee, was given "an airing" on the streets of Richmond. Her escort was a patriarchal-looking individual, Captain John Caphart. She was uniformed in blue cloth pants, frock coat buttoned up to the chin, a lady's black fur hat, and a pair of highly polished boots. Small in stature and pale in features, she forcibly reminded an observer passing her of an overworked factory girl, attired in the uni-

The Globe Tavern near Petersburg, Virginia, near which Jeb Stuart was killed. *National Archives.*

Miss Doctor Mary Walker—and her blue cloth pants. *National Archives.*

home with only the clothes they had on, and without food, seeking shelter wherever they could find it, and asking food of those who were able to give it to them. Contributions were collected for twenty-four of these unfortunate victims who were huddled together in a small house only a few miles from the city. The dwelling had been generously given up to them by a benevolent gentleman, the Justice of the Peace of Henrico. He himself was in limited circumstances, and could do but little else than give them shelter. As the days passed, many other refugees drifted into the city from battlegrounds held by the ar-

The battle of Petersburg, Virginia, June 16, 1864. From sketches by Edwin Forbes. *National Archives.*

form of a youth who had just discarded the roundabout. As she paraded the streets a goodly concourse of barefooted little Negroes noisily brought up the rear, highly amused at the free exhibition which was being afforded by permission of Captain L. W. Richardson, the commandant at Castle Thunder. Miss Walker had recently been quite sick, and the promenade was recommended to facilitate her convalescence.

The ostensible reason which took Miss Walker out was to lay before General Gardner, commanding the Department of Richmond, certain papers which she expected would secure for her permission to return home by the next flag-of-truce boat. She seemed anxious to make any concessions which might be demanded of her save that of her title and the right to attire herself in men's apparel. The General promised to consider her application at the earliest possible opportunity.

The Richmond press reported that the news from Maryland was encouraging. General Jubal Early and his jubilant Confederate forces were raiding the countryside and battering at the doorway of the Federal Capital. Before the Confederate Capital had time to

celebrate the event, Early and his troops were dashing in an opposite direction and Washington was still "in its place." More bad news for the Confederacy came with the reports that Atlanta had fallen into General W. T. Sherman's hands, to which a postscript was to be added later that his Yankee troops were on their way to the sea.

While the Stars and Stripes were flying over Atlanta, President Davis rushed to Augusta. Generals Beauregard, Hardee, Cobb, and several other army officers went with him. After hurried conferences, the President spoke to the citizens giving his reason for being there:

"At the moment of leaving your State, after having come hither to learn the exact truth as to the late military operations, I go away much more confident than when I came. I have been to the army, and return imbued with the thought that they are as fully ready now as ever to meet the enemy, and that if all who are absent will return, and those owing service will go, no foot of an invader will press the soil of Georgia.

"Never before was I so confident that energy, harmony, and determination would rid the country of its enemy and give to the

The Courthouse, Petersburg, Virginia. *National Archives.*

A teamsters' repair shop, Petersburg, Virginia. *National Archives.*

women of the land that peace their good deeds have so well deserved. Those who see no hope now, who have lost confidence, are the croakers, who seem to forget the battles that have been won and the men who have fought; who forget that, in the magnitude of those battles and the heroism of those men, this struggle exceeds all that history records. We commenced the fight without an army, without a navy, without arsenals, without mechanics, without money and without credit. Four years we have stemmed the tide of invasion, and today are stronger than when the war began; better able now than ever to repulse the vandal who is seeking our overthrow."

The President of the Confederate States of America had said the same thing a hundred different times in a hundred different ways. But on that day he was talking to "those who see no hope now, who have lost confidence" —and he was one of them.

In November, his message to Congress stated that he was opposed to making soldiers of the slaves. He said that the government had as many white soldiers as it was likely to

"The American brothers; or, 'How will they get out of it?' " *London Punch.*

require, or as it could conveniently support. He seriously recommended the purchase, from their masters, by the government, of the slaves then engaged in the service as teamsters, and others to the number of forty thousand instead of twenty thousand as had been suggested. He also proposed that the prospect of emancipation be held out to the Negroes thus employed as a reward for their good conduct. The masters were to be persuaded to allow them to remain on the property where they had lived as slaves.

The Richmond press never failed to publish reports of General Grant. True or false, he was always in the news. A Confederate soldier peeping over the Yankee line somewhere along the James River had seen one of their transport boats with its flag at half-mast, and returned to say that Grant must be dead. The rumor spread, but could not be verified. "The whole of summer has gone," wrote a reporter, "and neither Petersburg or Richmond has fallen yet. One thing is certain, dead or alive, Grant is keeping very quiet."

A few days before Thanksgiving another reporter had him back in the news. "The steady rains which produce fathomless mud, have put a stop to military operations," he began. "All was quiet, wet, and cheerless on Grant's lines before Petersburg and Richmond. Soldiers not on duty hung over their campfires in their bomb-proofs and log houses, and sighed for the return of fair weather. Now it

"The Bad Bird and the Mudsill." *Frank Leslie's Illustrated Newspaper.*

Ah! you may laugh — but if it wern't for this Mud I'd soon fetch you out of that ......

RICHMOND

seems doubtful that Grant was making ready for so early an advance upon our lines as we had all expected. He has gone to visit his family in New Jersey."

While he was there, enjoying Thanksgiving with his wife and children, the same reporter wrote that "turkey day was observed by Grant's army who, no doubt, devoured the several thousand birds sent them from the North. There was an unbroken quiet all along the lines from early morning until night." Richmond reporters were also commenting on Lincoln's recent re-election to the "Yankee Throne." One said that "the Abolition clubs in Washington went to Lincoln's White House on Thursday evening and, after firing off a cannon, proceeded to hurrah and hurrah until the Gorilla came out and made a pretty little speech."

An appeal to the public for aid in behalf of the families of soldiers and refugees in the city stated that Richmond was filled with sick war victims from every portion of the Confederacy, many of them the families of men on the battlefields. Liberal and regular contributions of money, food, and fuel were earnestly requested. The Southern Express Company had agreed to ship all articles contributed to the poor, free of charge. The proposition of providing a sumptuous Christmas dinner for the gallant soldiers of the army of Northern Virginia had met with universal approval. Other than liberal contributions from private citizens, the four branches of Congress and the General Assembly of Virginia, then in session in Richmond, voted one day's compensation for that purpose. Upwards of fifty thousand dollars had been raised.

A report on Christmas day that Lee was to be appointed generalissimo of the land and naval forces of the Confederacy, with all the power appertaining to that exalted office, was joyfully received throughout the South. "No act which the President could perform," said the press, "would have so great an effect in cheering and stimulating the country at this moment, when, above all others that have occurred, it requires cheering and stimulant." But the President did not make the appointment until February sixth of the next year, too late for the cheering and the stimulant.

Confederate breastworks defending Richmond and Petersburg were unoccupied and dreary during much of the winter. *National Archives.*

Tomorrow and Tomorrow

The last days of the Confederate States of America began with the New Year of 1865. The shadow of events to come was darkening the hopes and the spirit of a people deluded by leaders who were striving to hold up the props of a roof about to cave in. With few exceptions, when it crashed the leaders ran from under it, leaving the people pinned beneath the debris of their ambitions and the wasted blood of almost one hundred thirty-five thousand men. Never had the vultures of Europe hovered over a territory with such gleeful expectancy, waiting to pounce upon a divided nation when its life was spent. The future of an entire continent, and with it the world, was to be decided upon the battlefields that year.

Of the President, as the final hour drew near, the press had this to say: "Amongst those that are born of woman there beats not a bolder heart than that of Jefferson Davis. We are not ashamed to confess to a large amount of hero-worship for the man for whom his Northern foes can find no better name than rebel and slave-owner. Never unduly elated by success, never dismayed by adversity, his voice rings out clear as a trumpet call on the darkest day that befalls his country. Not Cato himself spoke to his little Senate at Utica with more dignity and steadfastness than does the Southern President when addressing his suffering fellow-countrymen. Four years have passed since the tremendous strug-

gle began with which his name will be forever identified; and, if American figures can be trusted (a point on which we always feel serious misgivings), those four years have witnessed a greater amount of bloodshed and a larger loss of human life than any other four consecutive years since the Deluge. The loss of ten thousand men on a single day has become quite a common event; and a conscription of one, two, or three hundred thousand at a time no longer excites astonishment. The wave of war has surged from North to South and from East to West. It has been waged by land and sea, on mid-ocean and in harbor, and up thousands of miles of river—in the midst of forests, on spacious plains, and on the sides of lofty mountains. Professional soldiers and amateur generals have tried their hands upon it; attorneys and politicians have brought their talents to its aid; every invention of modern times has been pressed into its service. Newfangled ships, cannon of hitherto unknown caliber, rifles of novel construction, new tactics and new tools, all have been used in turn, and yet the end has not come. Such energy, such obstinacy, such determination to win, have been shown on both sides as were hardly ever seen before, and such an amount of money expended as no other country ever spent in a period ten times as long.

"If, in the early days of this struggle, we were ever disposed to sneer at the efforts of either side, we must now, all of us, confess that we had underrated both their intentions and their probable performances. It is a struggle of heroic proportions on both sides. But, come what may, it is to the weaker party that the highest amount of admiration is justly due; and what is true of one is doubly true of the other. And now, after vicissitudes innumerable, the tide has turned of late against the South; and, doubtless, sore discouragement has fallen upon many a heart which not long ago was exulting in the sense of victory. It is not, indeed, a great many weeks ago since we were told, on what was assumed to be good authority, that discouragement was universal throughout the Northern States, and that the cry for peace—peace at almost any price—was upon every tongue. The result shows the folly of generalizing freely from particular instances, and yet only forty-eight hours ago there were many faint-hearted friends of the Southern cause in a state bordering on despair about its future prospects. So many men are ready to rush from one extreme to its opposite! But clear across the waters comes the brave voice of Jefferson Davis; there is no quaver in his tones—he speaks with no uncertain sound. Few as are

Confederate soldiers at a picket post. *Confederate Museum.*

his words reported to us, we cannot for a moment doubt his resolution; his voice is still for war! Dark as is the present hour, he has passed through hours as dark before, and through the gloom he believes he sees the coming dawn."

The press was not inclined to be ironical at that moment, confessed one reporter, and therefore refrained from the customary salutation of the season—"Happy New Year!" Such happiness as the season afforded, he added, could easily be carried in a nutshell, and "there are not wanting hammers to crack even the nutshell, and expel therefrom such withered kernels."

With all the pretentious boast of their leaders, the South was to emerge from the war scarcely as well off as the soldier who signed himself "A. B. C." in a letter to a Richmond editor. "The New Year's dinner has come and gone; or, rather, gone without coming. Some of the troops from the South seem to apprehend the Virginia troops being nearer home, may have gotten the best of them in the distribution. I think that, by stating the case of our regiment (the First Virginia, and enlisted in Richmond), this misapprehension may be relieved.

"I presume thousands of rebels, like myself, expected really a good treat to the inner man, and plenty of it, basing their expectations upon the colossal preparations in Richmond, the great number of Confederate dollars contributed by worthy and patriotic citizens, the glaring articles in the newspapers, and the names of the gentlemen who composed the committee, satisfied all of us that it would be a good thing; and, laboring under these impressions, we prepared accordingly, setting our incisors. The quartermaster and commissary were to have nothing to do with the sumptuous feast, nor were they invited to partake. Well, on Monday night notice was received at regiment headquarters to send a detail of men, with an officer, to brigade headquarters to receive our quota. (None of the committee have, as yet, made their appearance.) They soon returned with two barrels, holding the dinner. The contents were soon made visible by knocking in the heads. I will give you a list of the contents for the entire regiment, numbering two hundred and sixty men and officers: Thirty-two ordinary-size loaves of bread; two turkeys, one of them a very diminutive specimen of that species of fowl (some swore that it was a chicken); a quarter of lamb and a horse-bucketful of apple butter. Well, of course this immense weight of provender had to be divided out to the various companies. After our company had received its due proportion, the whole lot was, by unanimous consent of the company (numbering thirty men), condensed into six parts, and by a species of lottery, all thirty participating, the six 'piles' fell to six men; so twenty-four received *nothing*, and six *all*. I was on picket at the time, but found, upon my return to camp, that I was one of the successful six, and got the leg of a turkey and a half-pound of mutton, which I soon disposed of, with some fried bacon, red pepper, salt, water, and flour to thicken, making a French dish, which I leave for you to name. So ended our New Year's dinner. No blame is attached to any one. It was too great an undertaking, so say all the troops."

Winter had stalled military operations all along the lines in front of Petersburg and Richmond. But there was no peace in the expectancy of battle, and that was all the people of Richmond could look forward to in the silence of the guns at the moment. The only activity of the Yankees inside their lines, as seen by a Confederate soldier, was the building of winter quarters and the chopping of wood needed to supply their army. "Their quarters are nearly built," he observed, "and resemble large villages, looking very beautiful in their regularity *at a distance*."

Yankee raids had played havoc with railroads, and during the lull in fighting efforts were being made to repair them. Advertisements called for one thousand slaves to work on the Richmond and Danville Railroad, and three hundred slaves to work on the Piedmont Railroad. A Richmond home owner said that, contrary to all expectations, prices asked for the hiring of Negroes at the beginning of the year exceeded those of past months. As a consequence, only families compelled to have

help were engaging servants, but the streets were so crowded with idle Negroes that it was almost impossible to walk any distance without being jostled against them. Blockade runners on the South Atlantic and Gulf coasts had been able to get through and Richmond merchants published long lists of the goods they had on sale from that source. The Tredegar Iron Works gave notice to planters that they would exchange coal, iron, or nails, for corn, corn meal, hay, flour, beef, or bacon, needed to supply their ironworkers in Richmond and Western Virginia.

A special committee of the House of Representatives had been appointed to inquire into the causes of delay in the payment of soldiers and officers, and also in the furnishing of clothing to the army. Fortunetellers were reaping a fortune from confused citizens and soldiers trying to learn what was to happen to them during the coming year. One soldier paid a fortuneteller for advice and later discovered that his wallet was missing. "That a full-grown man, with a beard on his face, should be stupid enough to believe in the 'enchantment' of a dirty old hag, is beyond all comprehension," noted a reporter. "And yet men, and women too, support such characters and believe in their foreknowledge."

The Sisters of Charity of St. Joseph's Orphan

Harper's Weekly

JEFF DAVIS "CALMLY CONTEMPLATING."

"Our country is now environed with perils which it is our duty calmly to contemp *Extract from Davis's last Message.*

Asylum desired it to be distinctly understood that they had no accommodations for, and could not receive, foundlings. Several infants left at the door during the last twelve months had been handed over to the police to be conveyed to the city Almshouse.

The arrival of Francis P. Blair, Sr., from Washington by flag-of-truce boat, started various rumors in Richmond. The mysterious stranger was said to be at the Spotswood Hotel, then it was reported that he was at the home of Colonel Ould, commissioner of the exchange of prisoners. At first it was believed he had come with peace proposals, for he had been in conference with President Davis. When it was discovered that he was at Colonel Ould's home, it was thought he had come to settle the difficulty between the two governments relating to the exchange of prisoners.

After his departure from the city, the press commented that, no matter what his reason for being there, the Yankee had gotten nowhere and had been dismissed "with a flea in his ear." Before the end of January, Blair was back in Richmond, confusing everyone again. "Though we were not regaled with a glimpse of the venerable white-winged harbinger of peace, nor heard of anyone shaking hands with him at the President's House, his return indicates that he had been charged by President Davis with some communication which has not been made public, and that his first invasion might have been far more successful than has been supposed."

Again the city was full of rumors that President Lincoln and Southern representatives were holding a peace conference in Hampton Roads, that an armistice of ninety days had been agreed upon between the North and the South, and that a large white flag was already flying from the hostile lines below Richmond. Those who went out to see arrived at the moment it was being withdrawn, and the usual picket firing was resumed. They returned to Richmond with other news than that of peace. Grant was threatening another heavy movement near Petersburg; his troops were pouring in on the railroad from City Point; and some brisk skirmishing had occurred. A dispatch from General Lee, on the

Method of escorting officers, carrying communications between government officials of the North and South, through the lines by flag of truce. *Frank Leslie's Illustrated Newspaper.*

day he became Commander-in-Chief of the Confederate army, said: "The enemy moved in strong force yesterday to Hatcher's run. Part of his infantry, with Gregg's cavalry, crossed and proceeded on the Vaughan road —the infantry to Cattail creek, the cavalry to Dinwiddie Courthouse, when its advance encountered a portion of our cavalry, and retreated."

Every report gave some indication of approaching events. President Davis told Congress: "Our country is now environed with perils which it is our duty calmly to contemplate. Thus alone can the measures necessary to avert threatened calamities be wisely devised and efficiently enforced. Recent military operations of the enemy have been successful in the capture of some of our seaports, in interrupting some of our lines of communication, and in devastating large districts of our country. These events have had the natural effect of encouraging our foes and dispiriting many of our people. The Capital of the Confederate States is now threatened, and is in greater danger than it has heretofore been during the war. The fact is stated without reserve or concealment as due to the people whose servants we are, and in whose courage and constancy entire trust is reposed; as due to you, in whose wisdom and resolute spirit the people have confided for the adoption of the measures required to guard them from threatened perils."

The President then discussed what the Congress had, and had not, done—the currency, the exemption bill, even the peace conference between Lincoln and the Confederate representative in Hampton Road. It was his last message to that body.

On Washington's birthday, Richmond residents heard Grant's big guns, on lines below the city, booming a salute to the first President of the United States. The following day they boomed again in celebration of the capture of Charleston. On the third day some of the enemy's shells fell upon Petersburg and started an artillery duel which lasted several hours. Grant was believed ready for another dash at the Southside railroad. "Is he waiting for the roads to dry, for Sherman to come up, and for Sheridan to report?" asked the press.

The Federal Congress was considering a bill for the government of "the rebel States." The Confederate Congress had passed a bill to increase the military force by putting some three hundred thousand Negroes, between the ages of eighteen and forty-five, into the army. The Richmond City Council had recalled from the field all members of the fire brigade with orders to report to the Chief of Engineers at once. General Lee had made his last appeal to all Southern men who had deserted or were absent from the army to return immediately and promised that a full pardon would be granted them.

An arrival on a flag-of-truce boat said that Yankee gunboats, ironclads, and ships-of-war were off City Point, that the village had been enlarged to a respectable town, well supplied with machine shops, sawmills, and business houses. The wharves were very extensive, and the place was so changed in all respects that it could scarcely be recognized by those who had not been there recently.

"In view of the fact that our position as a people is critical," said the press, "it is respectfully suggested that all persons in the Confederacy observe Friday, March tenth, ap-

pointed as a day of fasting and prayer, with more earnestness and solemnity than has yet been manifested. It is proposed that all churches have at least three services, that the people eat no more food than is necessary to keep up their strength, that all light conversation be discarded, and that all amusement places be closed."

Near the end of March the news began coming in—intermittently, like the roar of the guns. The siege of Petersburg had begun! Between nine and ten o'clock Wednesday night (March twenty-ninth), the city of Richmond heard the sound of rapid and heavy cannonading in the direction of Petersburg. From parts of the city the blaze of the guns could be seen through the black and murky night. With every moment the fire quickened and increased, and continued to do so for more than two hours.

In Petersburg the entire community was aroused by the deafening roar of artillery and incessant roll of musketry, which shook every dwelling from roof to basement and caused the inmates to tremble with fear and alarm. Never, since the beginning of the war, had there been such a prolonged and terrible bellowing of cannon. The scene from Bolling's Hill was "more fearfully grand." For a distance of three miles, along the river, the horizon was illuminated with bursting mortars and exploding shells, while the line of battle was almost clearly defined by the sheet of flame from the muzzles of Confederate arms. The Yankees had attempted to burst through General John B. Gordon's lines. They came in swarms, sometimes several lines battle-deep, but were seven times repulsed with the most terrible carnage.

That same day, a heavy force of Yankees, consisting of cavalry, infantry, and artillery, headed by General Philip H. Sheridan, advanced by the Boydton plankroad toward Dinwiddie Courthouse. General Fitzhugh Lee attacked the raiding column of the Yankee forces and defeated it, capturing seven hundred prisoners. General Anderson, commanding the extreme right of the Confederate forces, attacked the Yankees on his front to ascertain their strength and their intentions

A Confederate attempt to regain the Weldon Railroad during the operations around Petersburg. Sketched by John Becker. *National Archives.*

for future operations. His forces met vigorous resistance and fell back; the Yankees did not pursue.

Monday, April third, the last day of publication of Richmond newspapers under the Confederate States of America, the press correctly predicated: "The most decisive, and it is feared the bloodiest battle of the war was begun last Friday in the neighborhood of Dinwiddie Courthouse, resumed on Saturday at Five-Fork road, near the Southern railroad, and again renewed yesterday at daylight on the immediate Petersburg lines. Yesterday the conflict was general along the Petersburg front from the Appomattox on the east, across the Weldon road and far to the west in the direction of Burkeville, and was waged throughout the day with great fury. We have

no particulars beyond those furnished by General Lee's dispatches, sent at intervals during the forenoon. From these it appears that his lines were forced in several places and that all attempts to re-establish them proved futile. We are left to infer that desperate efforts, resulting in an immense loss of life, were made in vain to retake them. There was some trifling success at different points, but insufficient to redeem the fortunes of the day. On the preservation of the Petersburg line of defense was believed to depend the safety of this city."

Lee could not hold the line and began to evacuate Petersburg, leaving the road to Richmond wide open. Sheridan blocked retreat at his front, Grant was closing in from the rear. On Sunday, the President was attending serv-

The capture of Petersburg. Raising the Stars and Stripes over the Customhouse, April 3, 1865. Sketched by Andrew McCallum. *Harper's Weekly.*

The Confederate Army as it stood on Conner's farm, at Appomattox Courthouse, Virginia, at the moment General Lee announced the terms of surrender, April 9, 1865. Sketched by Colonel Battersby. *Harper's Weekly.*

ices at St. Paul's Episcopal Church alone, his family having already left the city. A messenger arrived, handed him an official dispatch from Lee, and departed. Lee advised that he leave Richmond immediately. The President rushed back to the Executive Mansion, and, this time at least, followed Lee's advice without quibbling. Had Mr. Davis, instead of running away, gone to the Capitol, thrown open its wide doors, and, with pistols in his hands, belt, and boot tops, defied the Yankees, he would have been shot down, and his own blood spilled on a sacred spot to be forever marked in bronze as having been where he met a courageous and a noble end. But Mr. Davis, knowing as all men know that death comes someday, was not brave enough to grasp an opportunity which would have made him one of the most dramatic political characters in history. So, being what he was, Mr. Davis took to his heels.

Not realizing that the end was so near, the people of Richmond, hearing the roar of the guns, continued to hope that all was well. Then the roar became fainter and fainter as the guns moved farther and farther away. The people looked at one another. What could it mean? Suddenly the guns were silent. No one asked questions now; everyone knew the answer. For a moment the stillness that fell over the city was like the calmness of death.

Mr. Davis and several other high-ranking Confederate officials gathered records together and scattered to points of safety. As they fled from the city, government warehouses were set on fire and arsenals blown up to keep supplies from falling into the hands of the enemy. When the fleeing officials had crossed bridges, the bridges were destroyed to retard the enemy's arrival. But the people were left without protection against the criminals and the riffraff. It was a night of horror and pillage; drunks, thieves, and cutthroats roamed at large everywhere. No enemy ever was more welcome than the Yankees when they galloped into blazing Richmond to save the city and restore order. In less than six weeks, Jeff Davis was captured near Irwinville, Georgia, imprisoned at Fortress Monroe, then released under the general amnesty of December 1868. Twenty-one years later he died in New Orleans, and his remains were brought to Richmond for burial in Hollywood Cemetery.

The day after the capture of Richmond, Mr. Abraham Lincoln arrived by boat at a Rocketts landing. His son Tad, Admiral David D. Porter, and William H. Crook, a White House guard, were with him. They all walked through streets bordered by smouldering ruins to the Executive Mansion. The way was crowded with curious people staring at Lincoln, following him step by step. He talked with many of them, the Negroes calling him "de great Messiah." At the Executive Mansion, several Union officers, hearing of his arrival, called on him. He was shown about the house, and was amused by the remark of an old Negro servant left in charge of the place, who said that Mrs. Davis, on the day she departed, had demanded that he have everything in good order for the Yankees when they moved in. Before leaving Richmond, Mr. Lincoln and his party drove by carriage to the Capitol. From there, they returned to the boat, passing the prison storehouses of hate, and other buildings crumbling with bitter reminders of the long and bloody war.

On April ninth, in the home of Mr. Wilmer McLean at Appomattox, two weary men sat before a table in a little room. They had known the great expanse of battlefields, of long stretches of wide rivers, the hills and the valleys of a country both of them loved. Each man had a profound respect and consideration for the other, and for the troops and the people they represented. On the table before them were the terms of surrender—terms which granted to the victor no more than to the vanquished. There were no grand gestures, no bravadoes, no clanking of sabers. The two men spoke a few friendly words, and, each in his turn, took a pen in hand and signed his name to the document before him. One was Robert E. Lee, the other was Ulysses S. Grant.

In Richmond, as the flames cast their last weird shadows into the sky, the people began to speculate about their future. They gazed in silent bewilderment at the skeleton outlines of buildings, and the ashes of their city—the once-proud City of the Seven Hills. The sight, to them, symbolized a past that never would return. The South had fought for a way of life unknown in the North. The great majority of her people wanted to keep that way of life. Now they knew that the ghost of what had been would follow them throughout their lives, perhaps remain for other generations to face and try to fathom. Now they knew there was nothing more for them but an empty tomorrow,

and tomorrow,

and tomorrow,

and

(*Following page*)
Fires! Explosions! The Confederate Army and citizens flee the Capital as the Yankees arrive. *A Currier and Ives print.*

193

The flight of President Davis and his Cabinet. *Illustrated London News.*

A sudden alarm and stampede of Confederate officials escaping with government records and documents from Richmond. "Sketched on the spot by an English artist." *Frank Leslie's Illustrated Newspaper.*

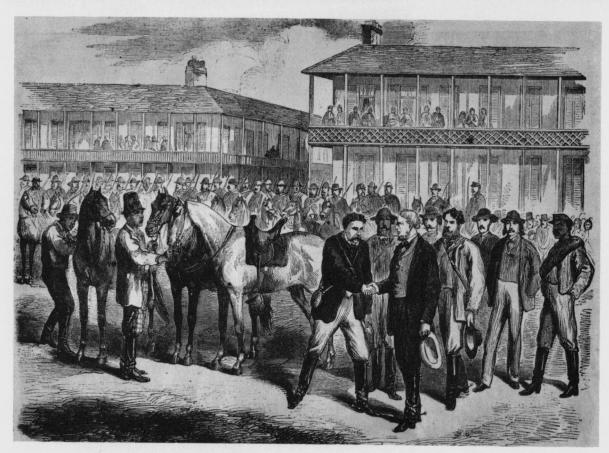

Jefferson Davis bidding farewell to his escort two days before his capture. *Frank Leslie's Illustrated Newspaper.*

General Sterling Price, C.S.A. (center), and other Confederates who escaped to Mexico City shown in a photograph taken there on October 9, 1865. *National Archives.*

April 3, 1865: The Union army enters Richmond, their drums beating and flags flying. The city still burns behind them. *Harper's Weekly*.

A Yankee commentary on the results of the War. The "inquiring stranger" asks, "Well, now the war is over, what are you people going to do for a living?" to which the "ex-slaves" reply, "Why, Master, we's gwine to draw." "Draw what?" "Draw rations, sir." The "ex-dominant race" on the right say, "I reckon we'll run—" "Run! After what?" "O! we'll run for offices of some sort—Congress, Legislature, Constable, or Notary Public, or anything!" *Frank Leslie's Illustrated Newspaper*.

April 4, 1865: Abraham Lincoln, President of the United States, walks through the streets of Richmond with his son Tad, Admiral David D. Porter, and William H. Crook, a White House guard, on the way to the Executive Mansion only days before occupied by Jefferson Davis. *National Park Service.*

"President Lincoln enters the late residence of Jefferson Davis in Richmond, Virginia; sketched by special artist, Joseph Becker," reads the caption on this old print. *National Park Service.*

The once-proud City of the Seven Hills. A view of ruins from the south side of the Canal Basin. *Library of Congress.*

The destruction of the Richmond and Petersburg
Railroad bridge delayed Yankee troops and supplies
from reaching the city. *Valentine Museum*.

Skeleton outlines of buildings stood in graveyards of debris after the flames had passed and the echo of the last explosion had torn through the city. *National Archives.*

Surrounded by ruins, the lamps on Carey Street wait to light the way again. *Virginia Historical Society*.

Row after row of Confederate guns captured by the Yankees lined the banks of the James River at Richmond. *Valentine Museum*.

The Capitol (upper left) and the Customhouse (center) were only slightly damaged, but the fire took a heavy toll of surrounding buildings. *Library of Congress*.

Confederate guns were everywhere—and silence. *National Archives*.

Bricks from the towering Arsenal littered acres of ground after it exploded. *Library of Congress.*

Negro refugees, with their household possessions, lived on canal boats until shelter could be provided for them on land. *Virginia Historical Society.*

"Richmond ladies on the way to receive United States government rations: 'Don't you think that Yankee must feel like shrinking into his boots before such high-toned Southern ladies as we?'" *Cartoon by A. R. Waud in Harper's Magazine.*

The Freedmen's Bureau in Richmond was established to take care of former slaves. *Frank Leslie's Illustrated Newspaper.*

A group of freedmen on the canal bank in Richmond at the end of the War between the States. *Valentine Museum.*

Index

DATE DUE